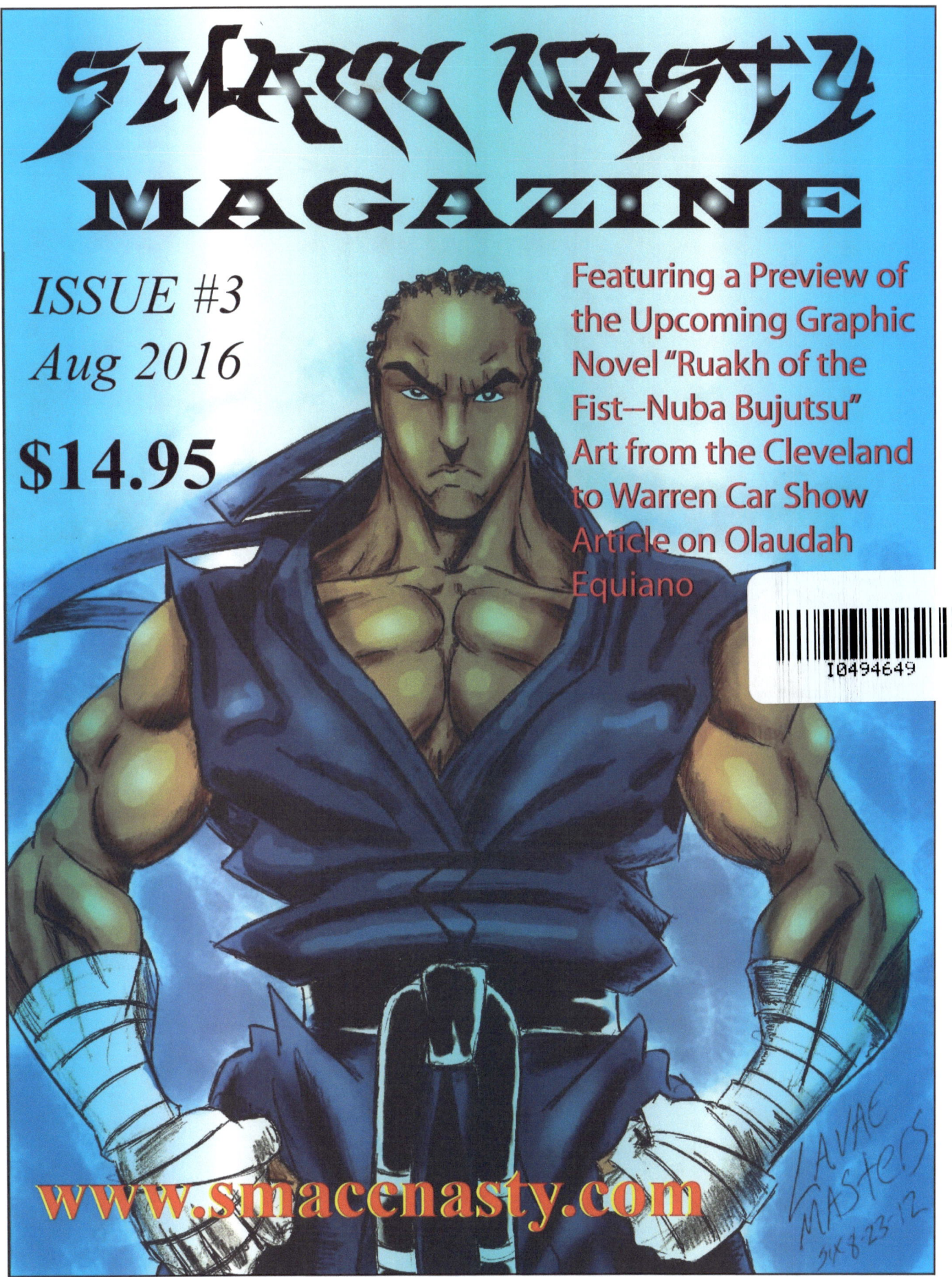

SMACK NASTY
MAGAZINE

ISSUE #3
Aug 2016

$14.95

Featuring a Preview of
the Upcoming Graphic
Novel "Ruakh of the
Fist—Nuba Bujutsu"
Art from the Cleveland
to Warren Car Show
Article on Olaudah
Equiano

www.smacenasty.com

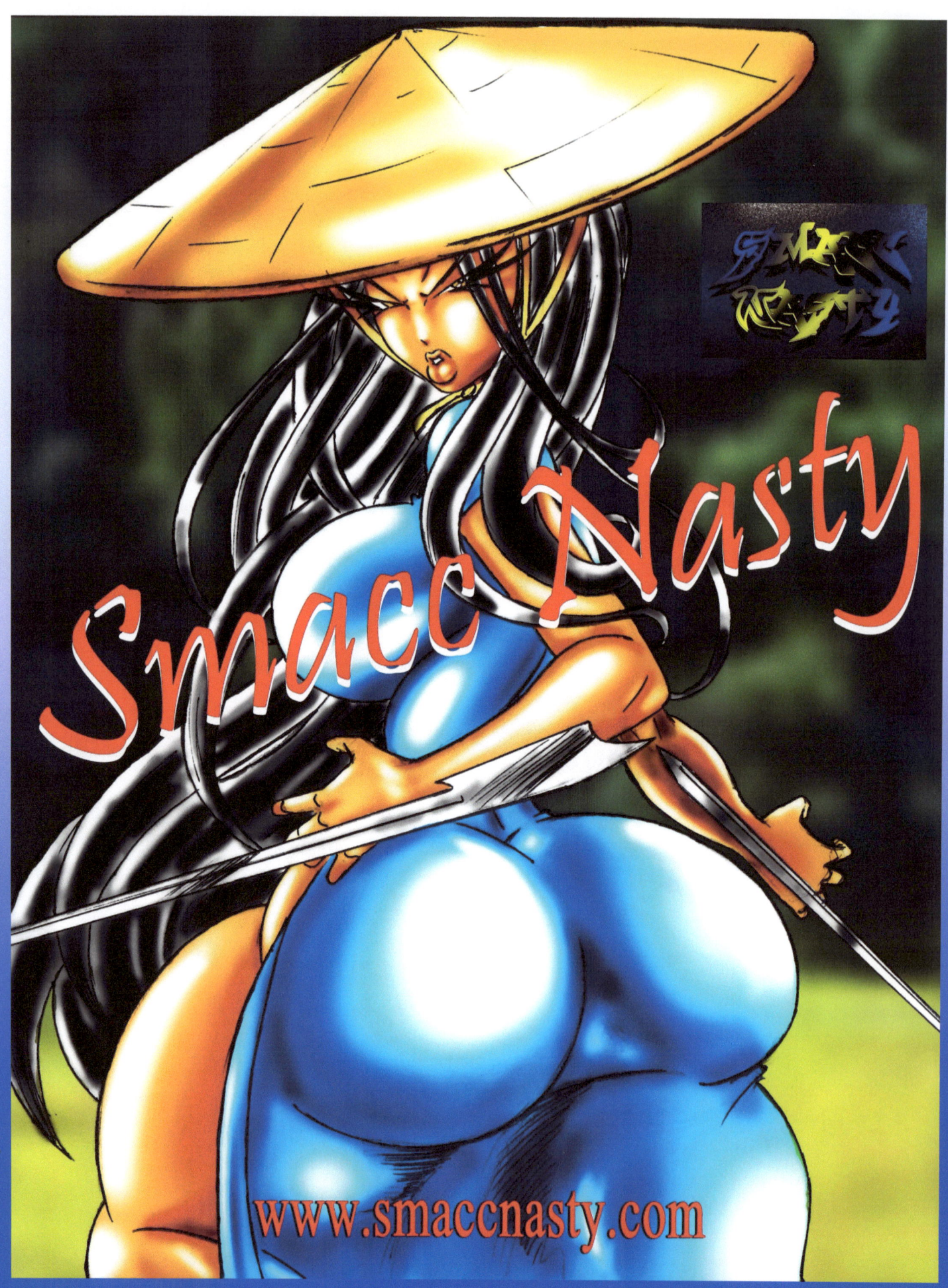

Table of Contents

Auto Body Artist

Sacramento, California is the home of one of the greatest and hard working auto-body artist in the country. Willie "Big Steve" Reed works diligently everyday restoring and repairing the pride and joy of our lives. Our cars. For many of us our wheels are not just a mode of transportation, but it is a reflection of our very inner beings. Big Steve helps people to bring out the reflection of our souls as we insinuate our presence on the mean streets and highways of this diverse country. His work definitely qualifies as "Smacc Nasty"!

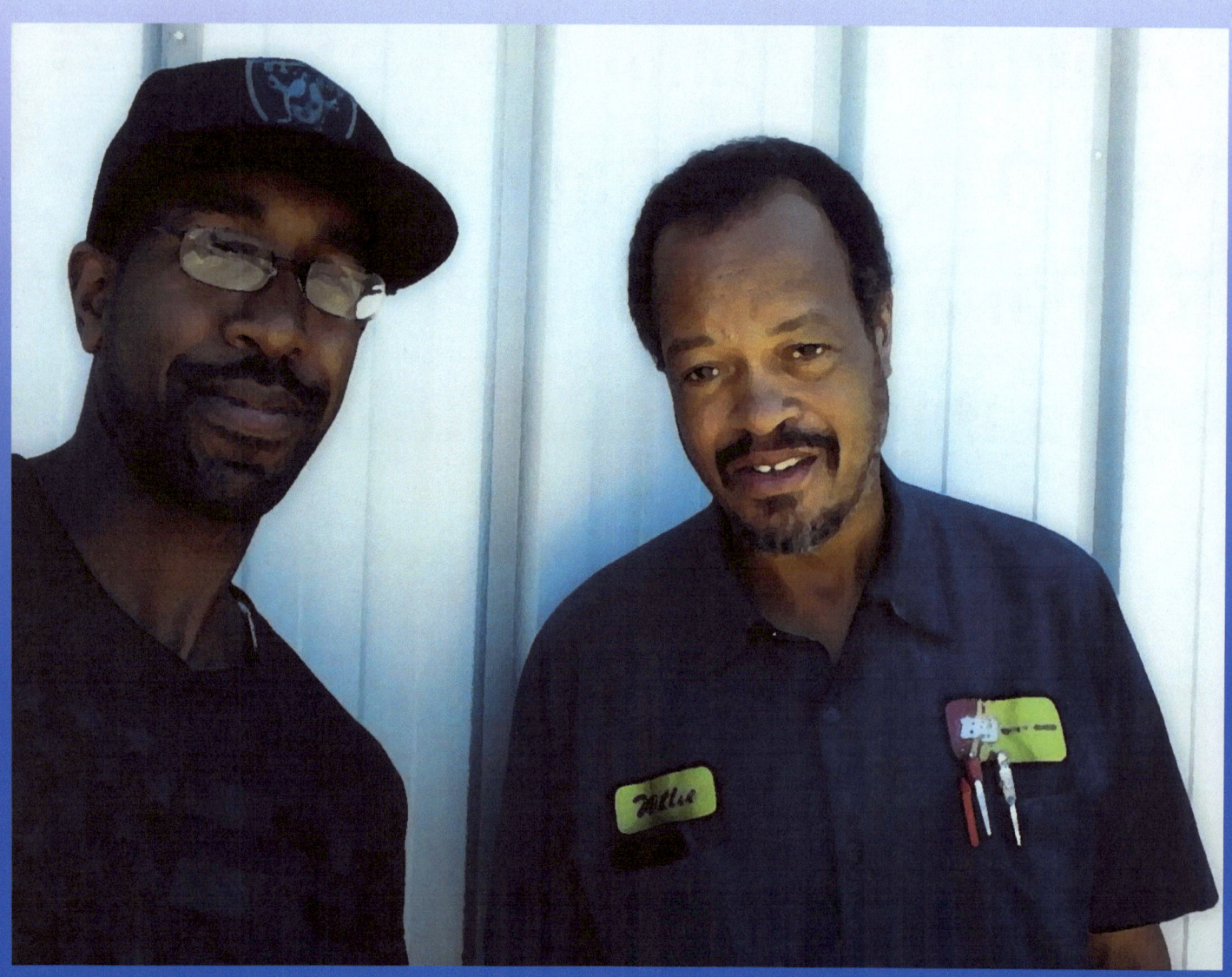

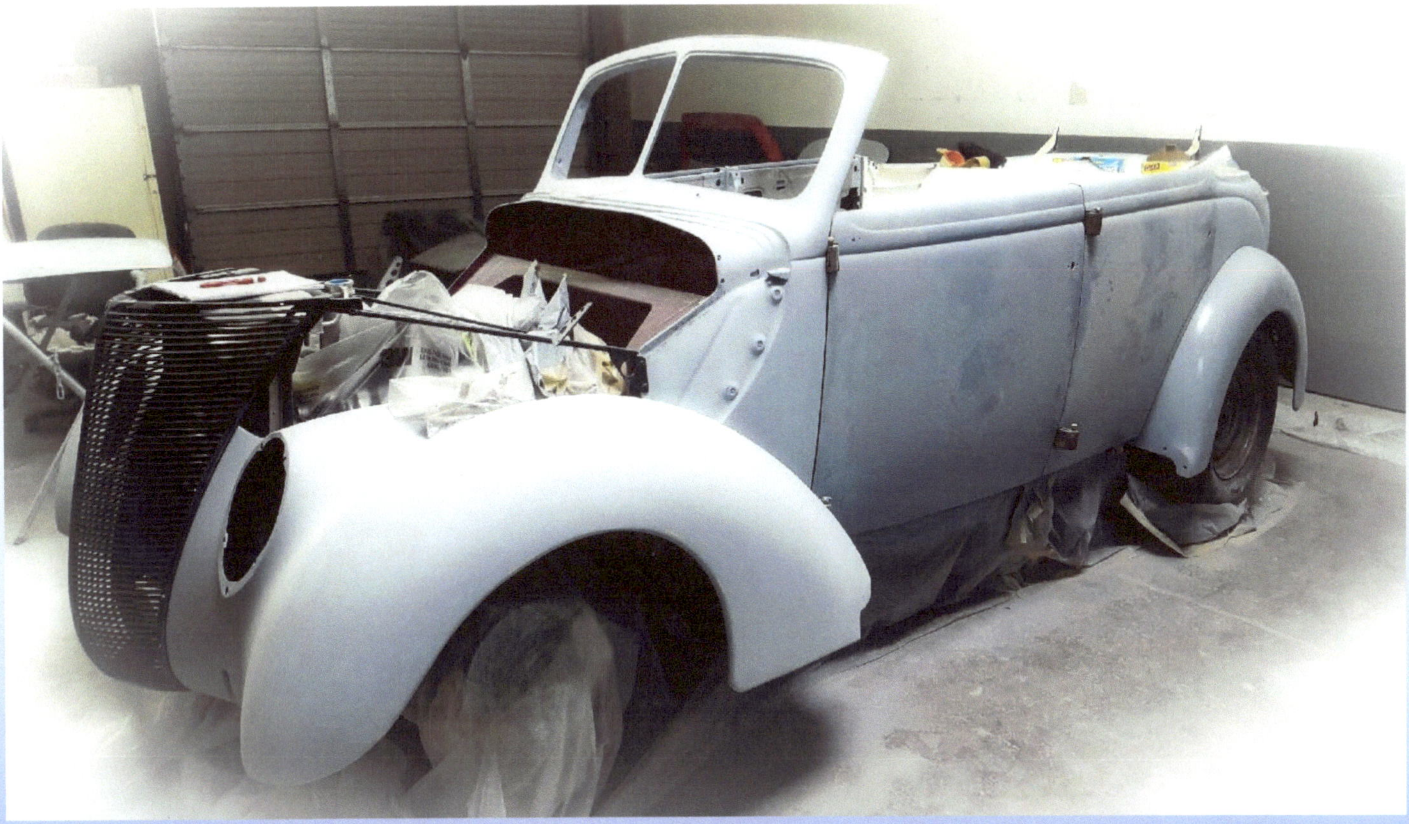

Big Steve's Auto Body Work

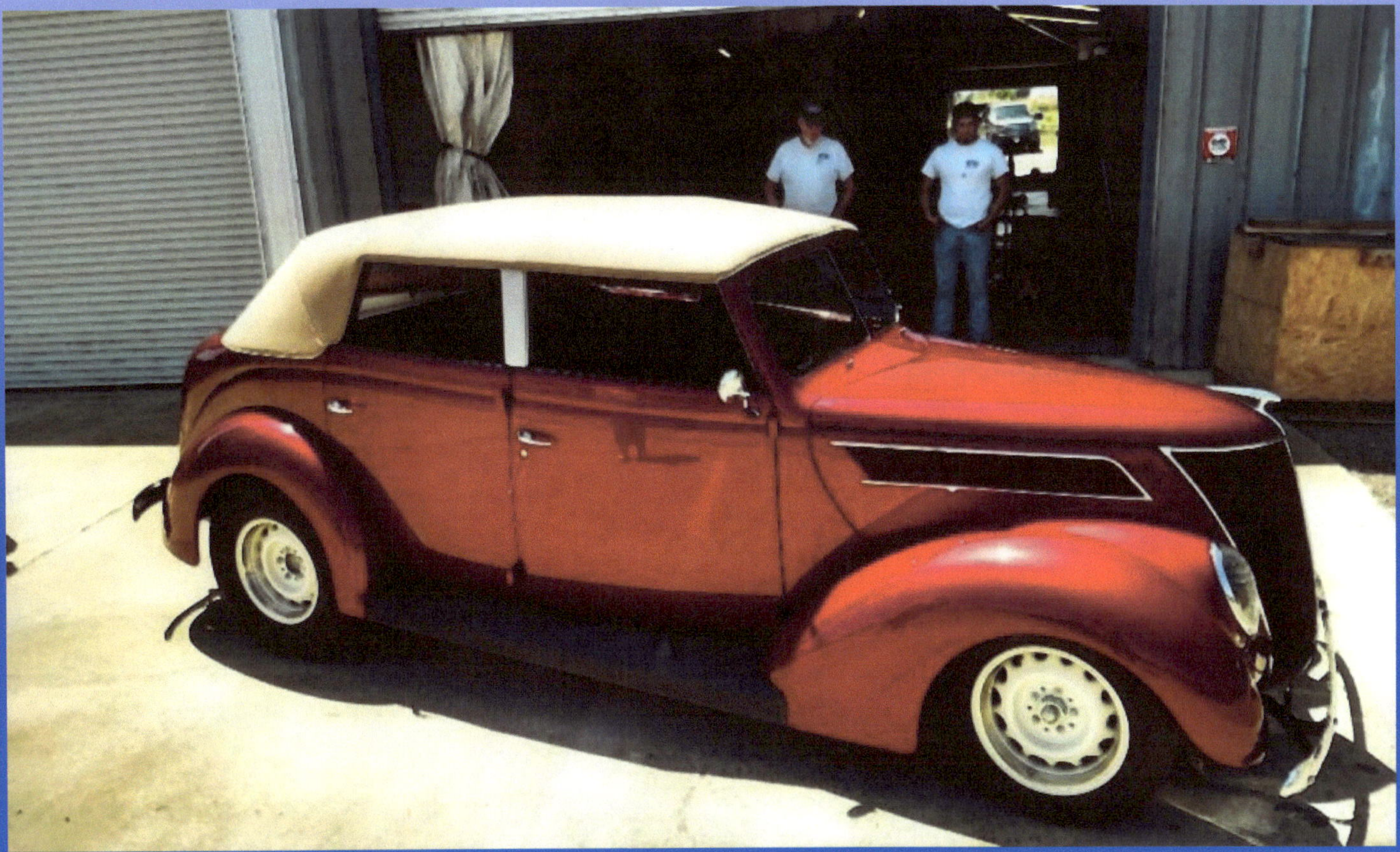

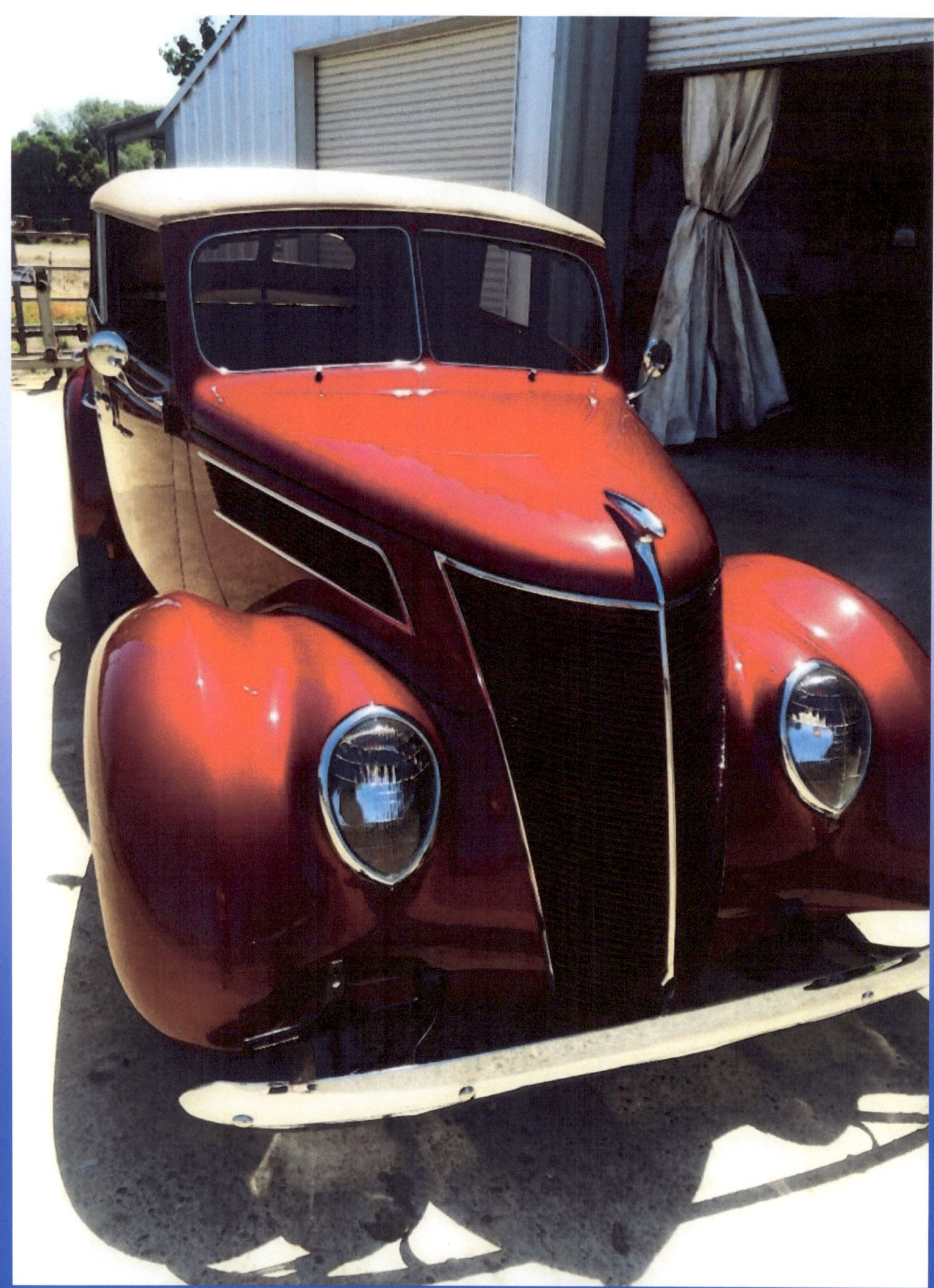

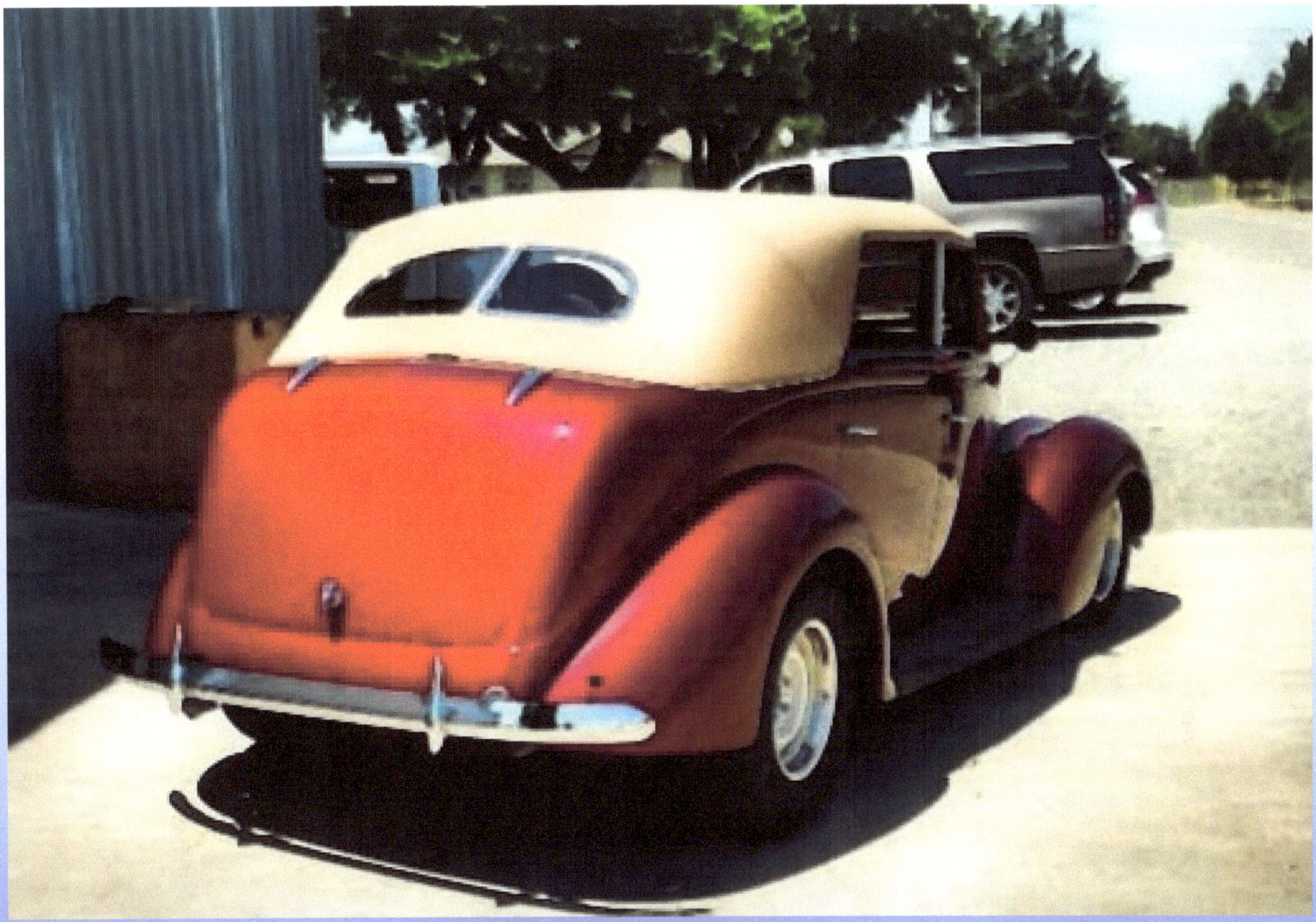

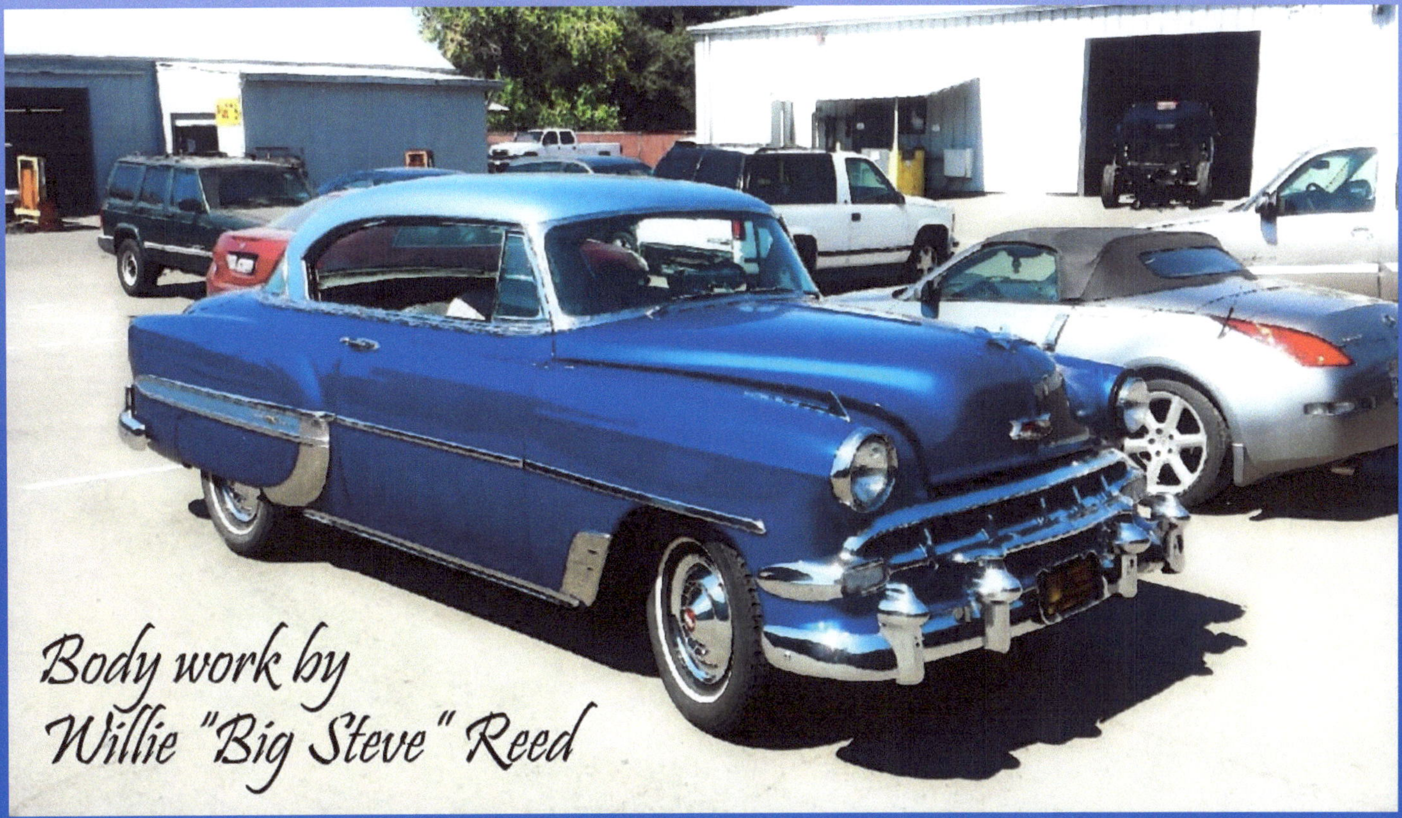

Body work by
Willie "Big Steve" Reed

Smacc Nasty Corporation travels to Warren, Ohio to attend the Cleveland to Warren Car Show. Check out the whips and wheels our photographer captures; eye-dazzling, Smacc Nasty rides.

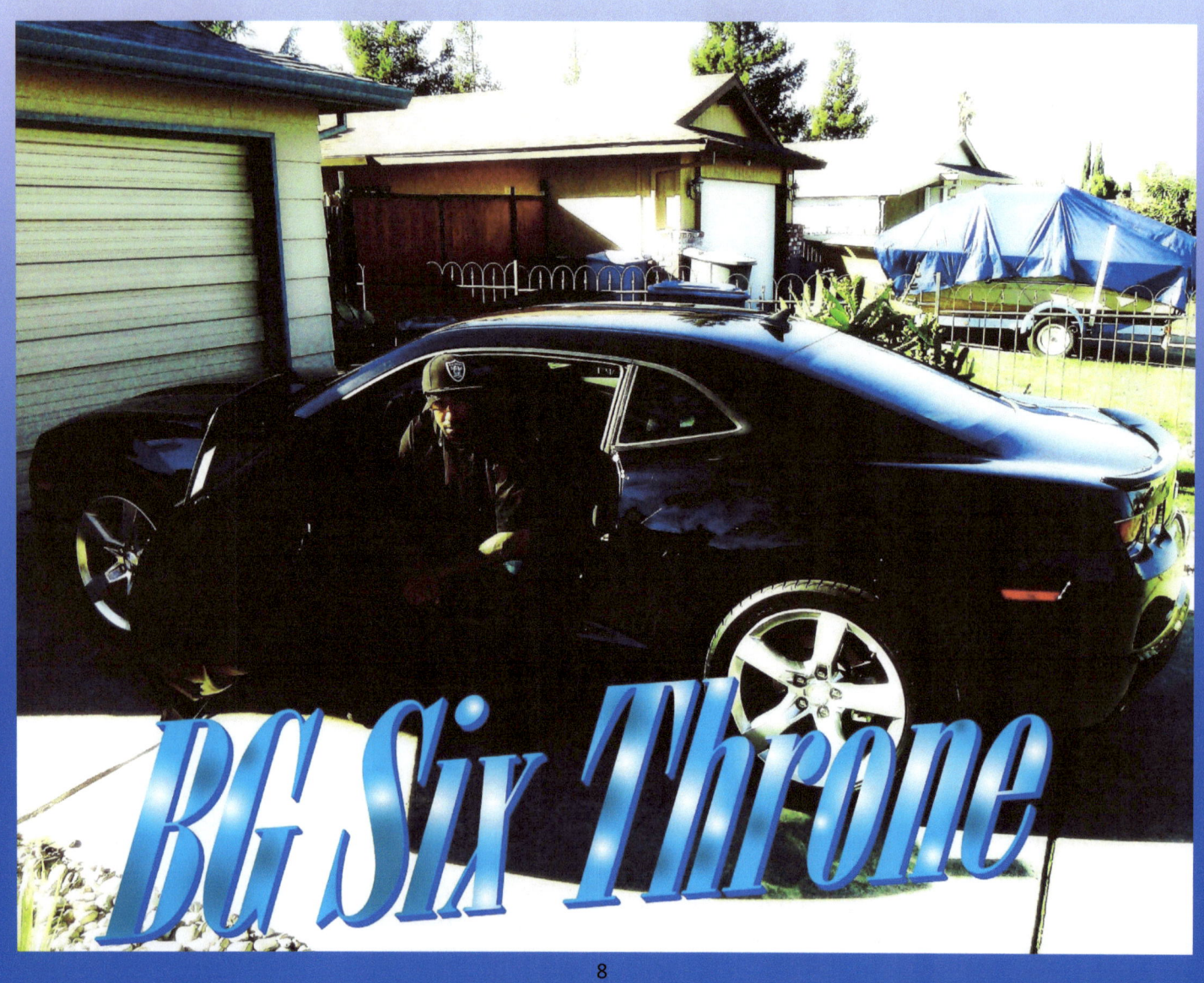

Cleveland to Warren Car Show

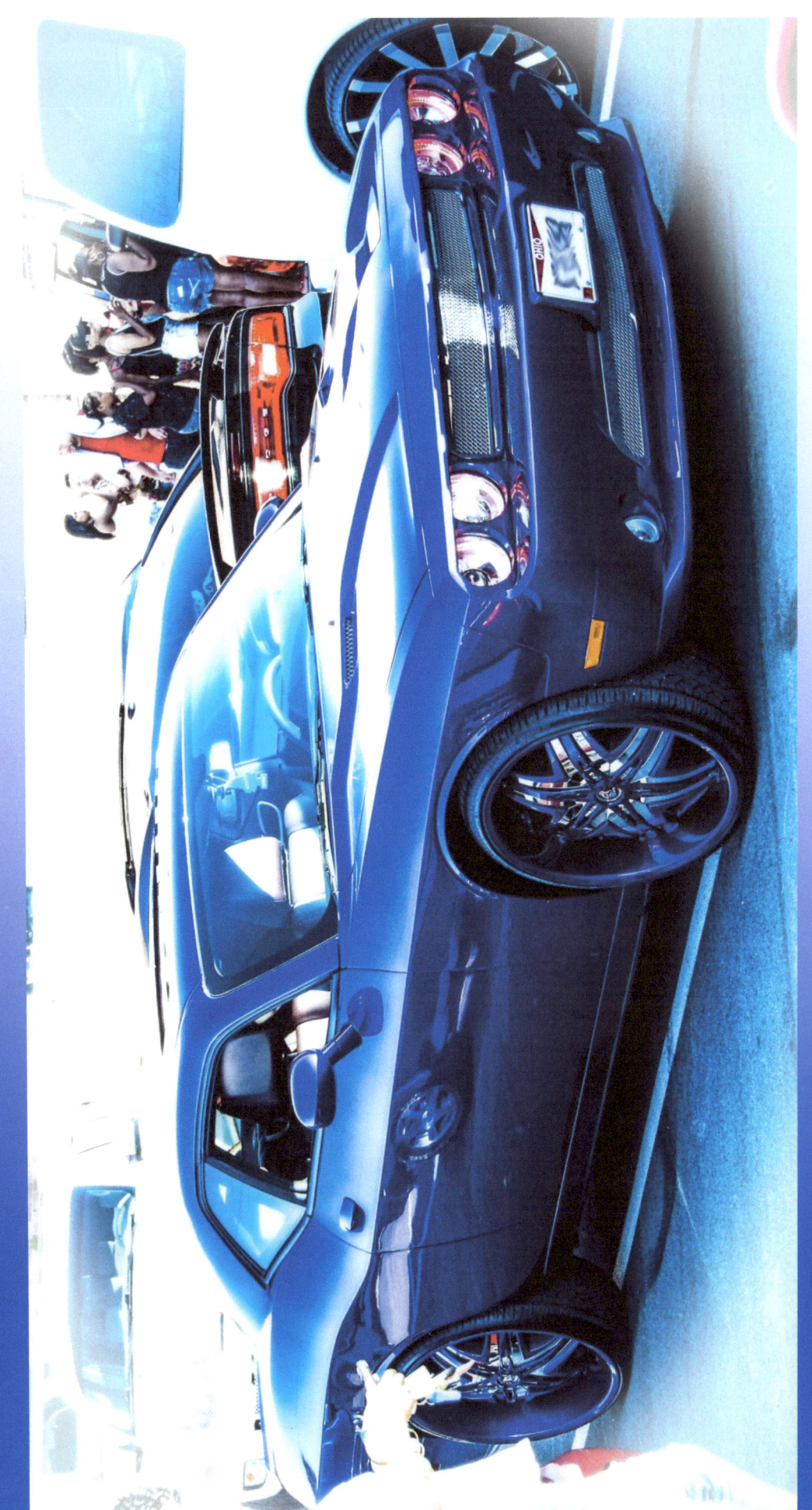

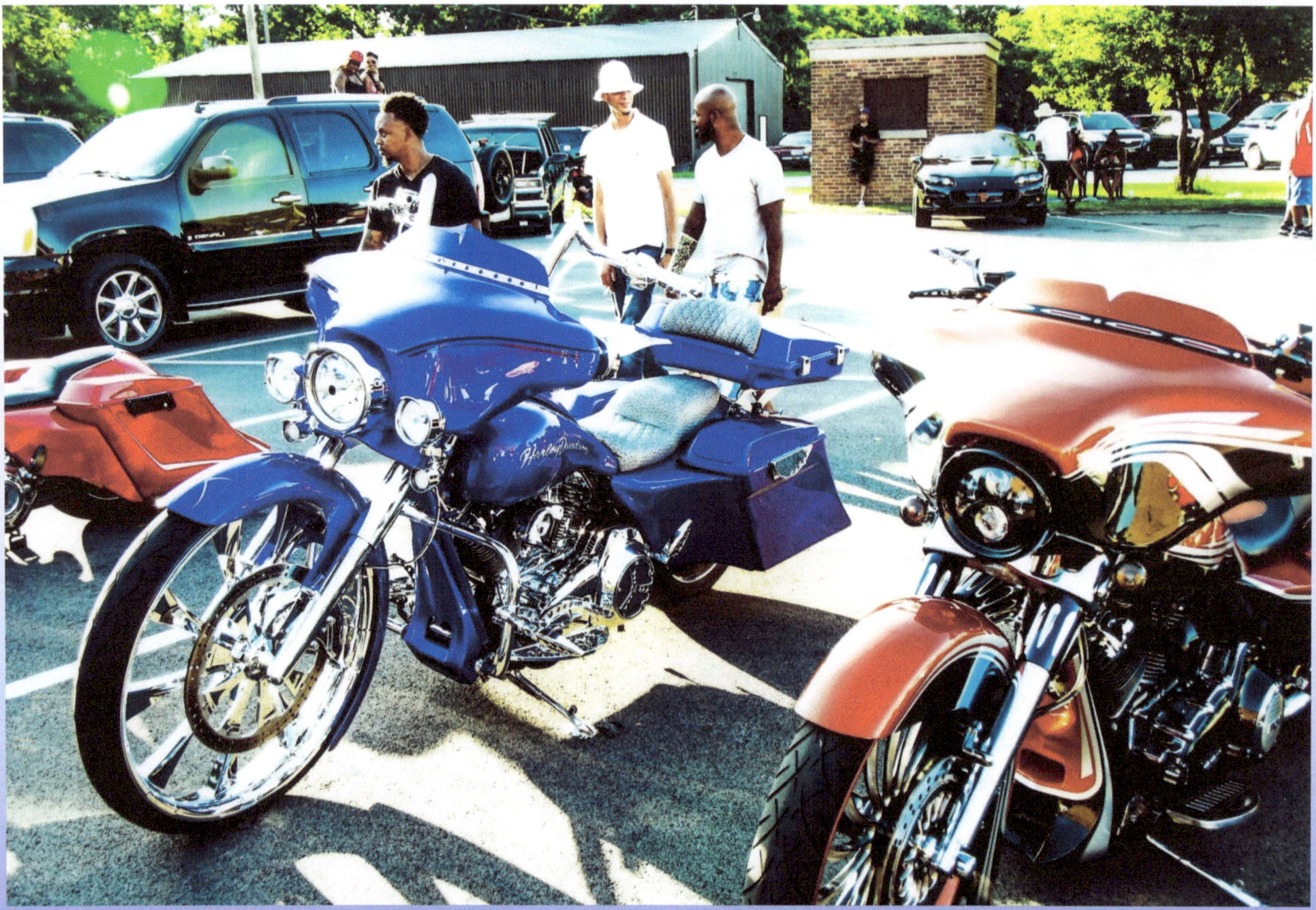

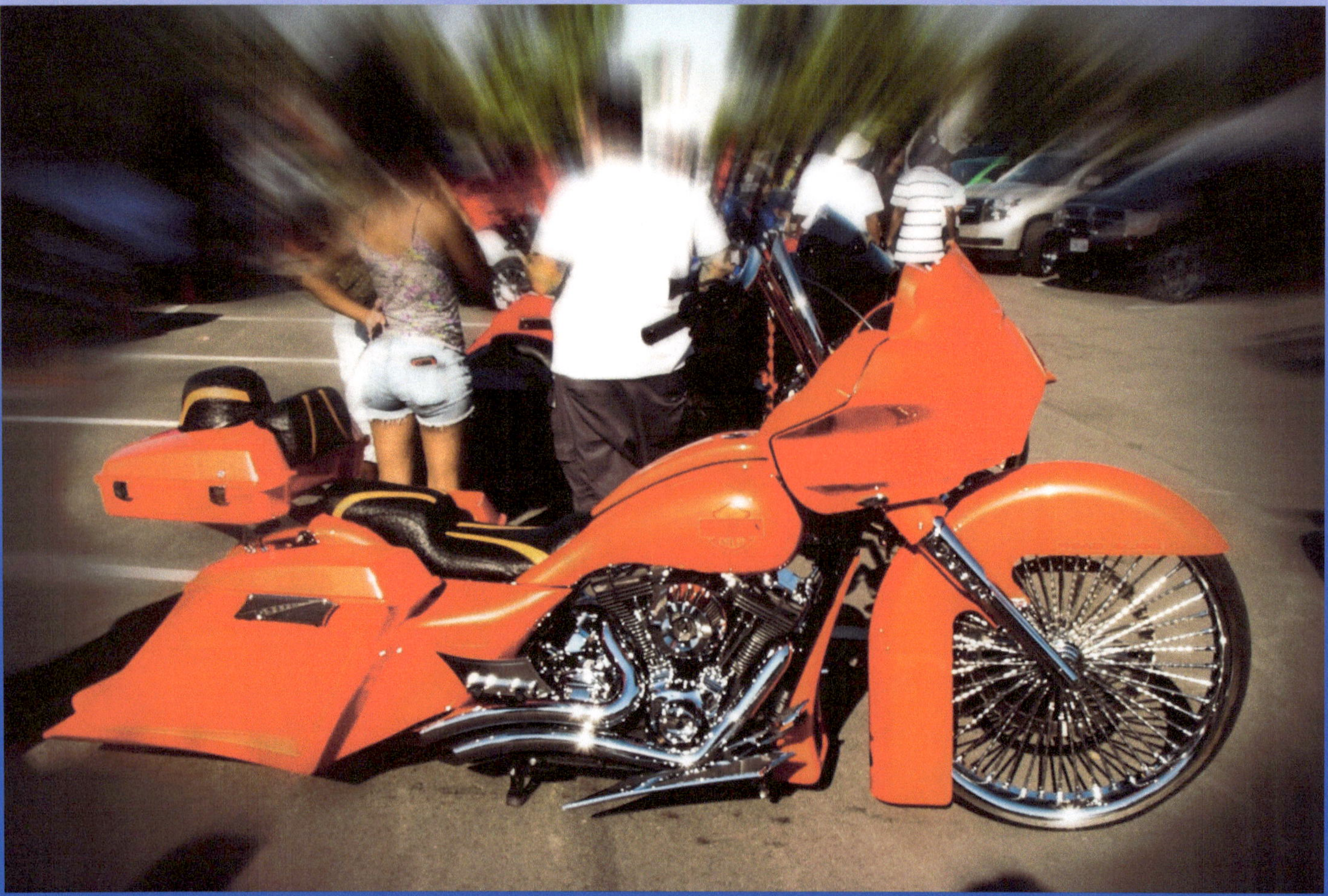

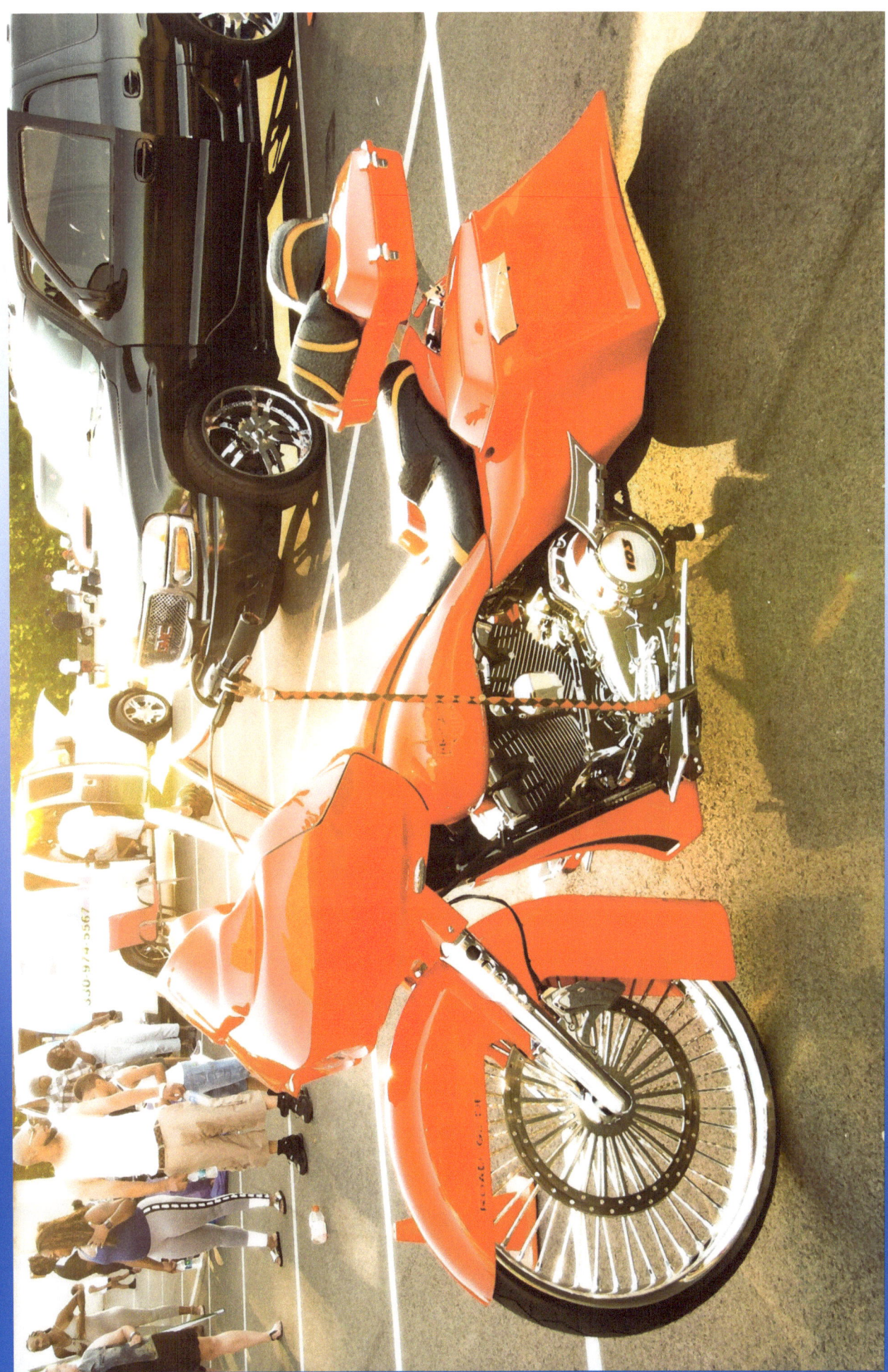

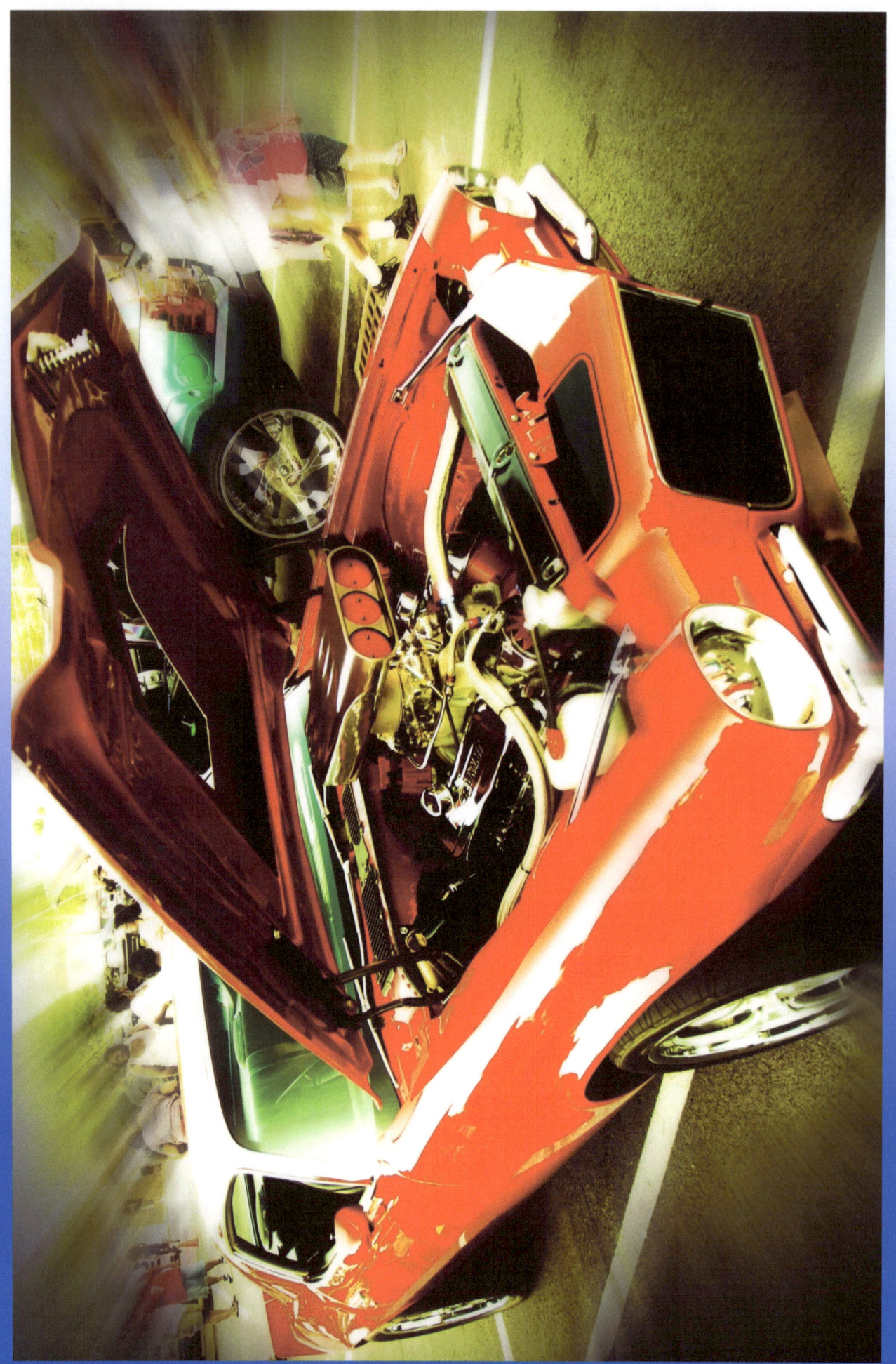

Photo by Yehezqel Ben Yisrael

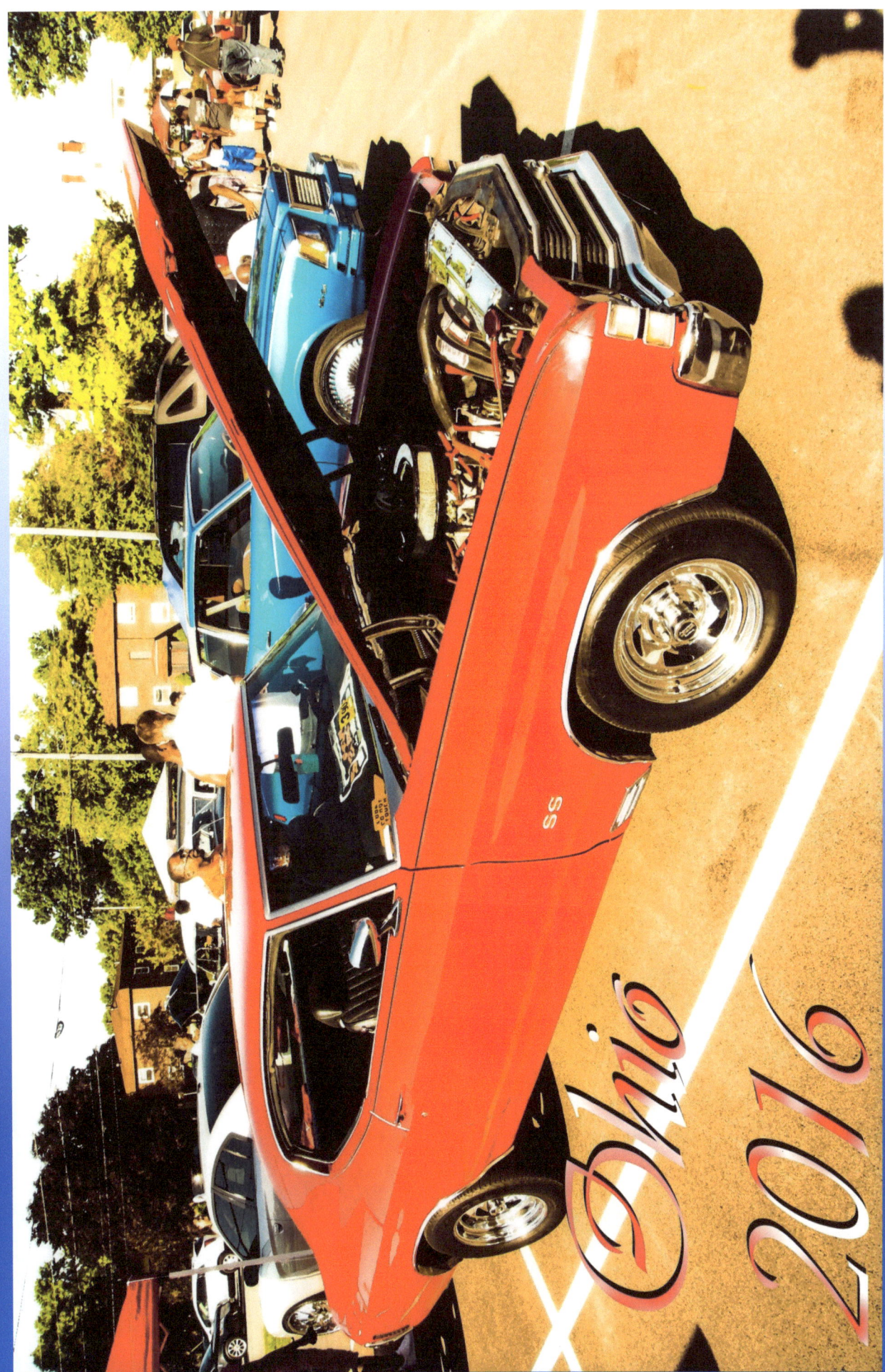

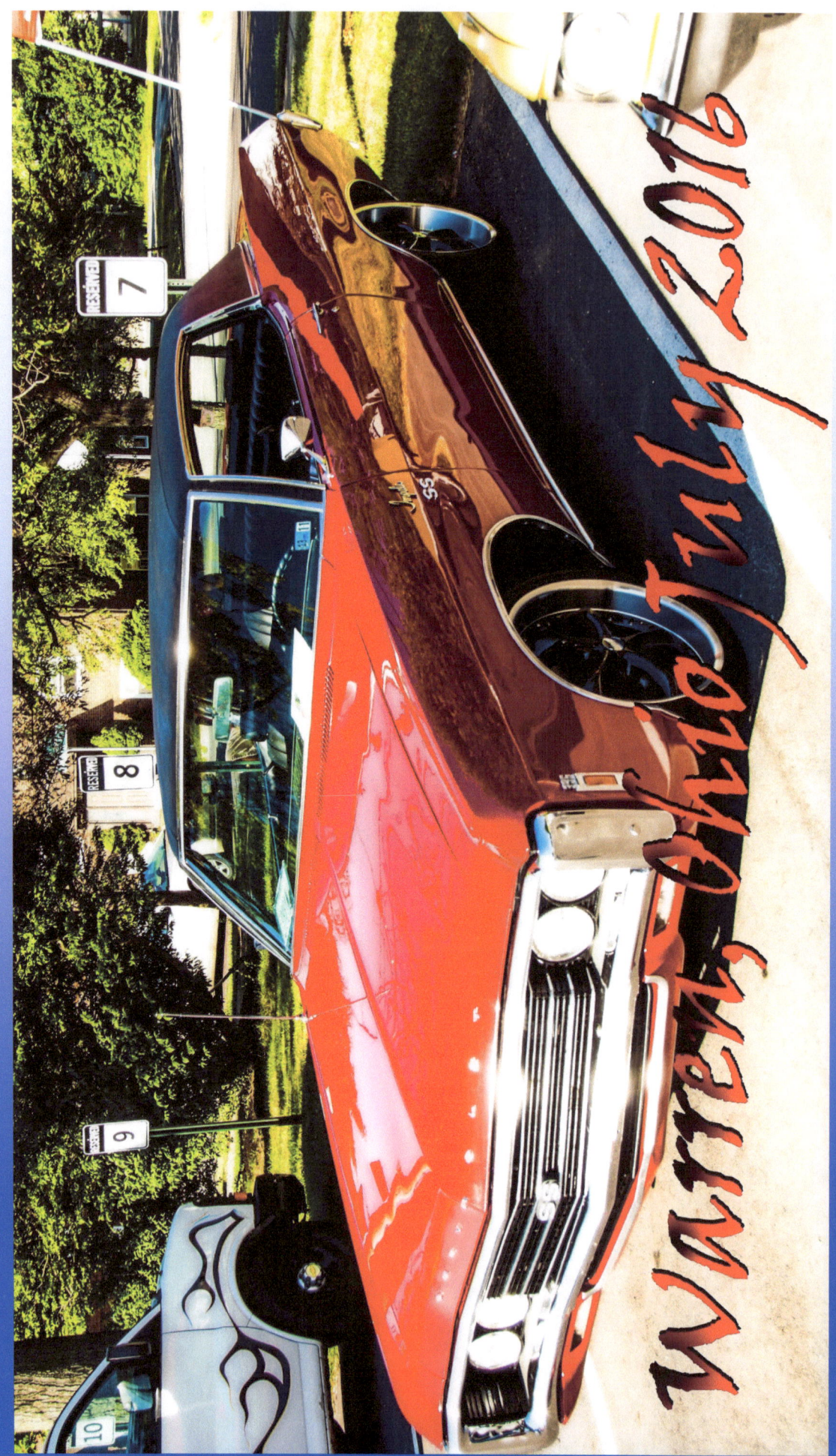

Warren, Ohio July 2016

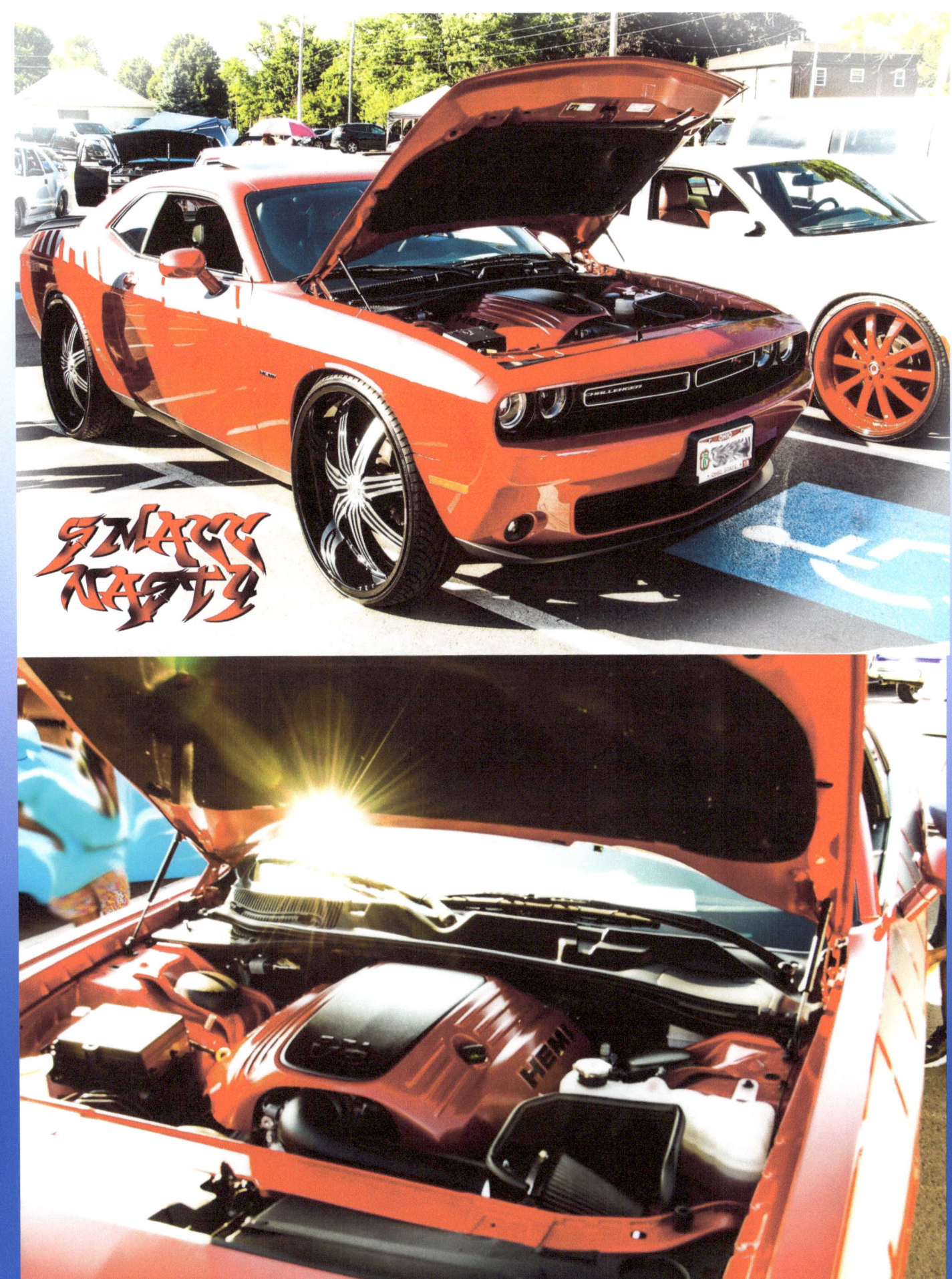

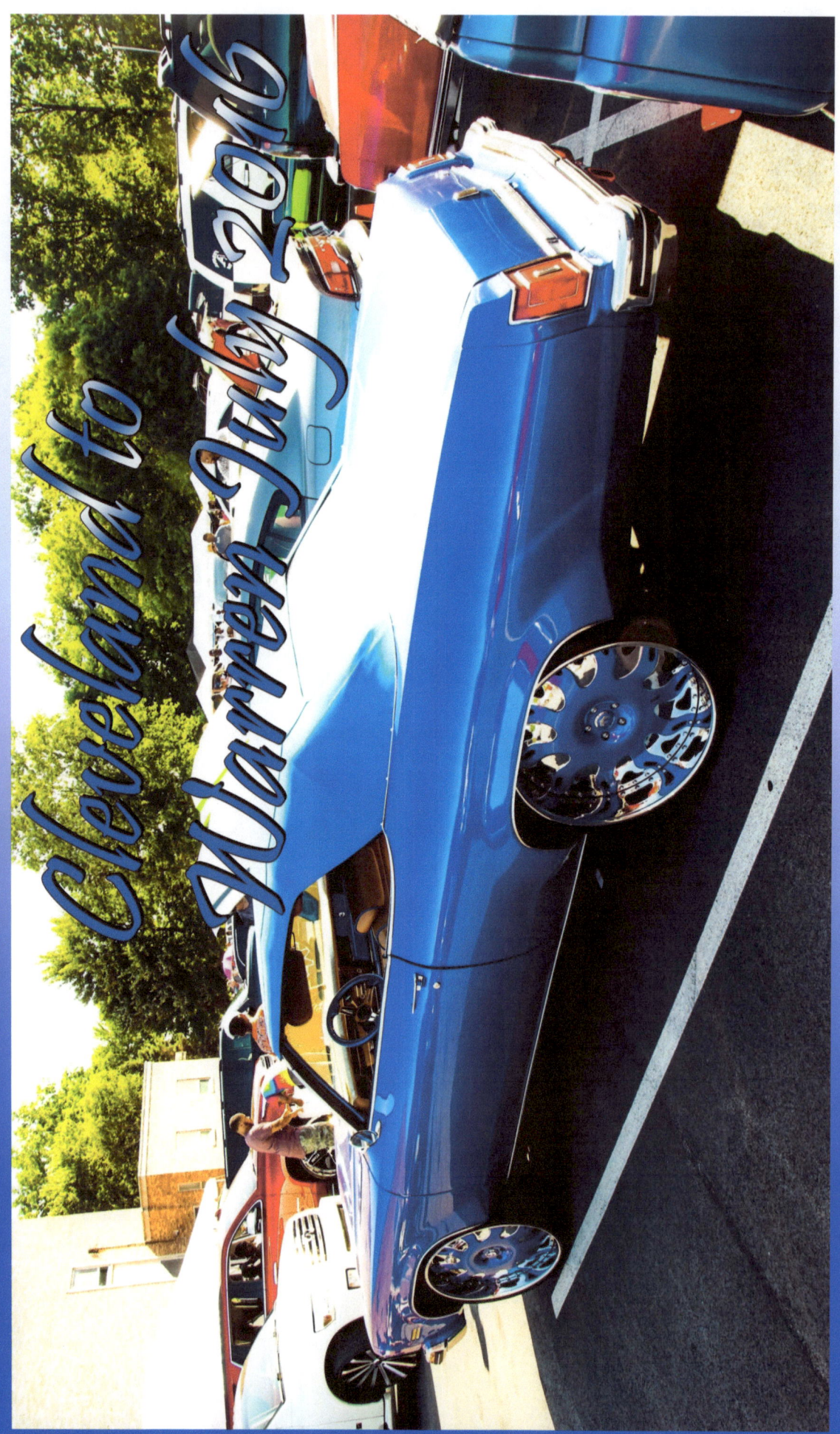

Cleveland to Warren July 2016

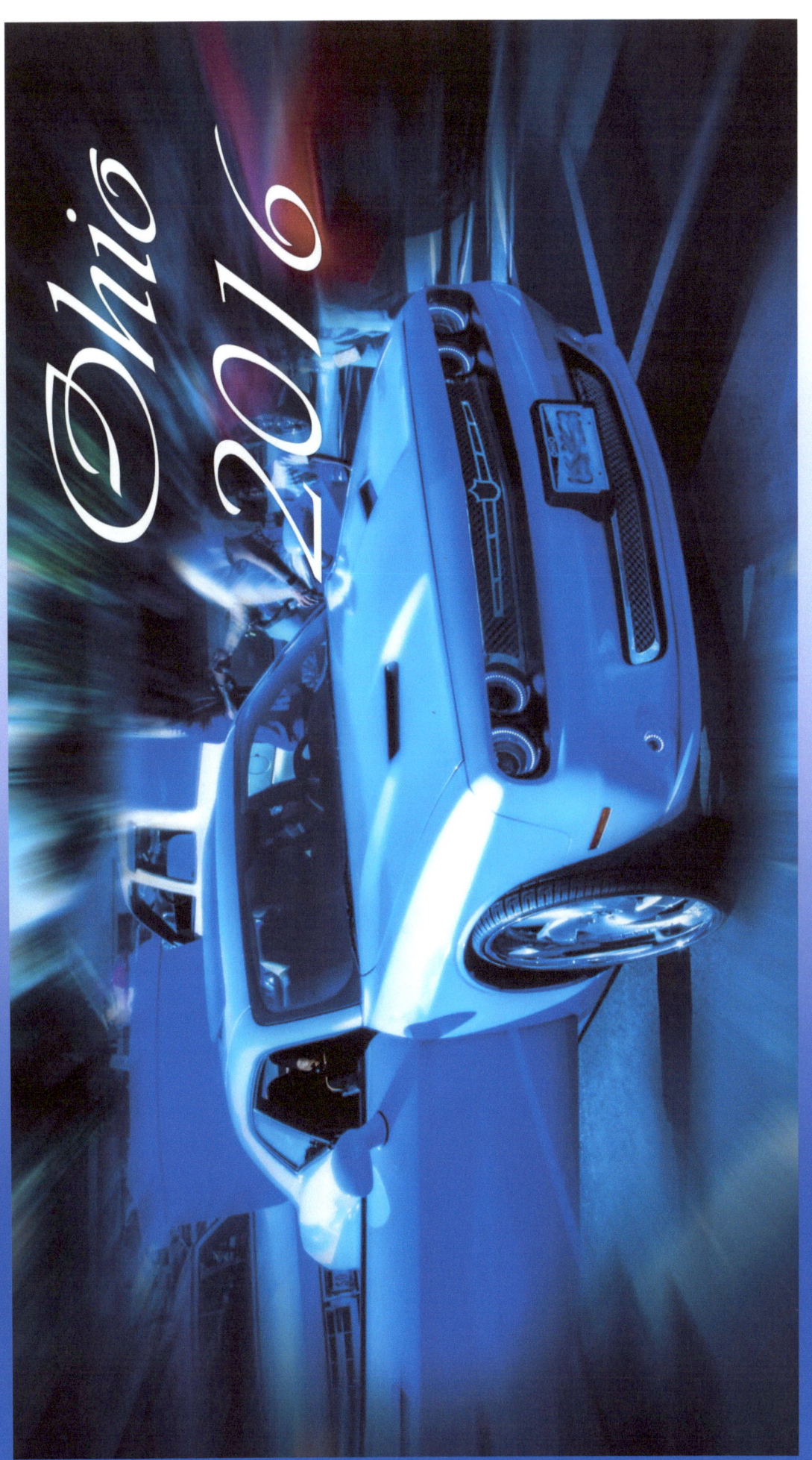

Cleveland to Warren Car Show

Photos by Yehezqel Ben Yisrael

A Perspective on
Olaudah Equiano

By Yehezqel Ben Yisrael

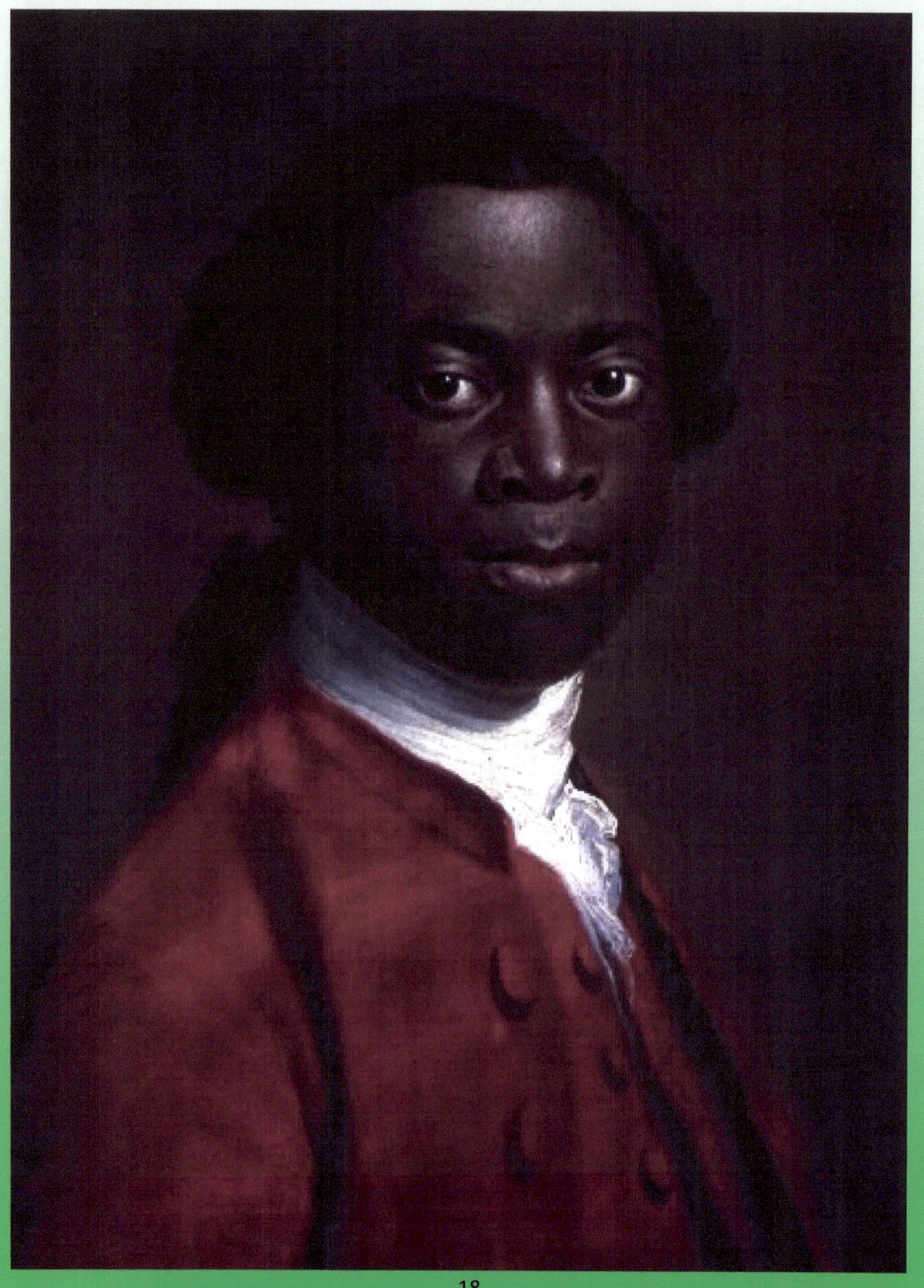

Religion: what role did it play in the telling of the story of Olaudha Equiano, who was

also known as Gustavus Vassa, the African? Religion played a significant role in the life of

Gustavus Vassa the slave who was born in Africa. Indeed, religion played a major role in the

lives of many people during the time of Olaudah. Olaudah was born approximately 1745. The

Life of Olaudah Equiano states that he was "an Ibo from northeast Nigeria". The Ibo people

are polytheistic, meaning they worship many gods. This is the notion of many that have read

this book. Also, some assert that he was a Muslim, that somehow he was of the Islamic

religion and that he worshipped Allah. Others believe that he and his tribal family were into

practicing divination or that he is actually descended from the biblical characters Abraham

and his wife Keturah. Still, others believe that he is actually a descendant of Abraham through

his third wife Sarah, who later gave birth to Isaac, who brought forth Jacob, who brought forth

Judah, the theorized forefather of Olaudah Equiano. Evidence will be presented that will

support the last statement; Olaudah was indeed from the tribe of Judah, which some people

today call the "Jews" of Africa.

"I regard myself as a particular favorite of Heaven, and acknowledge the mercies of

Providence in every occurrence of my life." (Equiano,9,10). Providence is known as the

protective care of God or nature as a spiritual power.   The Ibo's believe in a supreme god

called Chukwu. According to Judaism the Hebrew word "Chukma" is the spirit of the God who created the Heavens and the Earth. It is interesting to point out that the Ibo language is derived from a group of languages found in West Africa. In the year 65 B.C. the Roman armies under General Pompey captured and destroyed Jerusalem. A few years later in 70 A.D. General Vespasian and his son Titus put an end to the state of the Jews with great slaughter, humiliation and destruction. During the period of the military governors of Palestine, many atrocities were committed against the remnant of the people. During the period from Pompey to Julius, it has been estimated that over 1 million Jews fled into Africa, running away from Roman mistreatment and slavery. The slave markets were full of black slaves that were Jews, or more correctly, Yahudim. This is proof that Hebrew speaking Jews were scattered into Africa, hence a mixing of languages over the years as they assimilated into the nations of Africa. Olaudah's name displays the history of the mixing of languages and as to what tribe his Ibo family truly descended from. Yahudah is a tribe of Israel; the same tribe that the Romans persecuted in the above quote. The ancient Hebrew that was spoken by the Jews can be found in many West African countries today, including the Ibo. Although the Hebrew language has been corrupted through mixing into other languages, many similarities in word style and usage is prevalent in the Ibo language and many other African languages. Olaudah comes from the word Yahudah. "I was named Olaudah, which, in our language, signifies 'vicissitude or fortunate'", (Equiano, 18). Yahudah in Hebrew is loosely translated as praised or fortunate.

The mannerisms, culture and tribal structure of the Ibo is almost exactly of that of the ancient Hebrews of Abraham, Moses and King David's time. The ancient Hebrews appointed judges or chief men within their families to settle disputes and to enforce the laws of the tribes. "Those Embrenche, or chief men, decided disputes, and punished crimes." (Equiano, 11). In the government of the Hebrews adultery was punishable by death, if proven in court, but if a woman was only suspected of adultery her husband would divorce her. The next man knowing of her divorce would not dare marry her, leaving the woman to be a servant or slave. "Adultery, however, was sometimes punished by slavery or death; a punishment which, I believe is inflicted on it throughout most of the nations of Africa." (Equiano, 11). Even the arrangement of marriages by families of their children is comparable to that of the ancient Hebrews. "Both parties are usually betrothed when young by their parents…Sometime after (sometimes years later) she is brought home to her husband, and then another feast is made…Her parents then deliver her to the bridegroom, accompanied with a number of blessings (gifts of value)." (Equiano, 11). The dietary standards were also strikingly similar to that of the Hebrews. "Bullocks, goats, and poultry." (Equiano, 13). Indeed, most Africans did not eat pigs and scavengers of the sea; this was learned from Europeans during slavery. All of the descriptions that Olaudah gives of his family lifestyle lines up with what the Jews call "halakha" or the way of ones walk., though there are some differences, which will be addressed shortly.

The Ibo and the ancient Hebrews have similar personifications of their idea of God. "As to religion, the natives believe that there is one Creator of all things, and that he lives in the sun…" (Equiano, 17). The Hebrews also believe that their god is the Creator of all living things and that his presence is as strong as the sun in its full strength. Olaudah speaks about the belief that their god governs events, such as deaths and captivity. The Hebrews also believed that God has an appointed time for everyone's death and he decrees the enslavement and captivity of nations of peoples. "And the Lord shall scatter thee among all people, from the one end of the earth even unto the other; and there thou shalt serve other gods, which neither thou nor thy fathers have known, even wood and stone." (Deuteronomy 28:64, Bible). The Jews understood that this was a future prophesy from the time of Moses that the Israelites would be scattered into the nations of the world (Africa, Asia, and Europe) and be made to worship wood and stone; the wood representing the cross or Christianity and the stone representing the kaba stone, which in Islam is understood to be a piece of the moon. In ancient times, before the Prophet Muhammad, Arabs worshipped many gods, but their principle diety was the moon, which they called Allah. And today they still worship Allah, but through the efforts of the Prophet Muhammad, Allah is now their only god, and he is still symbolized by the moon (i.e. images of the crescent moon on their flags), but they believe as the Jews and Christians that there is one God and that he is the Creator of all living things. We will see shortly that Olaudah did not nor did he ever serve Allah, so therefore to say that he was a Muslim is incorrect. But alas, he converted to Christianity, to serve the wood, as the prophesy of Deuteronomy decrees.

Concerning more traditions of the Ibo that parallel the customs of the ancient Hebrews is that of the usage of their calendar system. "We compute the year from the day on which the sun crosses the line, and, on its setting that evening, there is a general shout throughout the land...and hold up their hands to heaven for a blessing." (Equiano, 17, 18). The Jews have a custom to blow a rams horn, shout and have a celebration at the beginning of their new year called Rosh Hashanah. The ancient Hebrews based the beginning of the day by the rising of the sun, while the modern Jews say that the beginning of the day begins at sunset. What is most striking is that the Ibo practiced circumcision. "We practiced circumcision like the Jews, and made offerings and feasts on that occasion in the same manner as they did." (Equiano, 18). Another tradition that Olaudah recollects was that of cleanliness, like in the manner of the Jews. "I have before remarked that the natives of this part of Africa are extremely cleanly. This necessary habit of decency was with us a part of religion, and therefore we had many purifications and washings; indeed almost as many, and used on the same occasions, if my recollection does not fail me, as the Jews." (Equiano, 18). Olaudah himself makes many remarks as to the ways of his Ibo family being comparable to the Jews. Why does he do this? Probably because it is the closest religion that he can compare it too. While Muslims have many similar customs they do not hold their feast on the same days as the Jews and the eating of camels by Islamic peoples is not comparable to the Jews or Olaudah's Ibo family. Another comparison to be made of that of the ancient Hebrews and that of Olaudah's tribe is the offices of priest and wise men and not having public places of worship. Before the Hebrews built there temple in Jerusalem, they were wonderers among many different nations, so they usually worshipped their creator from their tents. During and after the time of Moses, the priesthood, which was the tribe of Lewi called all the shots for all twelve tribes of the families of Israel. The word of the prophets or wise men was to be obeyed and never disregarded. "Though we had no places of public worship, we had priests and magicians, or wise men." (Equiano, 18). The Hebrew priest even had methods of discovering if a jealous husband had good reason to believe his wife was cheating on him, even when the jealous husband had no evidence to present. The same can be found in Olaudah's Ibo tribe: "They had likewise some extraordinary method of discovering jealousy, theft, and poisoning." (Equiano, 19).

Later in Olaudah's life he is presented with teachings from the Holy Bible from the perspective of Christianity. "There was one Daniel Queen…this man soon became very much attached to me, and took great pains to instruct me in many things. He taught me to shave, and dress hair a little, and also to read in the Bible, explaining many passages to me, which I did not comprehend." This is a very sad quote, for Hebrew men do not shave their beards and they do not seek instruction of God from foreigners. It is clear that the rich heritage of Olaudah's forefathers is being thrown aside to practice foreign doctrines, which was of no benefit to him; however he was keen enough to see the similarities of Christianity and the laws of his own land. "I was wonderfully surprised to see the laws and rules of my own country written almost exactly here."

It is a well-documented fact that the Hebrews are responsible for the writings of the "Old Testament" of the Bible and that the New testament was added later by the Romans almost 300 years after the Hebrews were scattered out of the land of Israel. Not a single Hebrew was present at the council of Nicea in 325 AD, but only Roman bishops and politicians—white men, who came to the conclusion that the writings that make up the New Testament should be added to the Hebrew sacred scrolls, an act in itself that is forbidden by the Hebrew scrolls.

It is obvious that Olaudah and his family were once a part of the tribe of Yahudah, but because of war and persecution they fled into Africa and made a new home with the tribes of the nations of Africa, namely the Ibo. Being a part of the Ibo tribe, Yorubas, Hausas, or Ashantis has nothing to do with genetic family traits or DNA, but is more about a collection of neighboring African tribes who come together out of necessity for survival. Today, people try to give African Americans DNA test to suggest what tribe they come from in Africa. This bit of science has problems. A DNA test can tell you who is your father and who is not, but how is a DNA test going to tell someone what group did their father associate with? That is like someone getting a DNA test and the results show that they are a Republican or a Democrat. This is the kind of foolish thinking that Olaudah fell into with the brainwashing of his slave masters who influenced him with Christianity. "After our vessel was discharged, we soon got her ready, and took in, as usual, some of the poor oppressed natives of Africa, and other Negroes". What other Negroes is Olaudah referring to; a native Ibo, Yoruba, or Ashanti, or an Ibo, Yoruba, or Ashanti that has origins from somewhere else, perhaps Israel or Arabia?

Olaudah in his own words, many times tries to make deals with God and he is indeed taken in by what he sees as miracles. Christians make a fine habit of chasing after miracles and the occurrence of what they perceive to be miracles they use as justification for their faith, while Hebrews are trained and conditioned to obey the commandments of their creator; hence, the benefits and increases are a result of their obedience to the laws of their God. "All my sins stared me in the face; and especially I thought that God had hurled his direful vengeance on my guilty head, for cursing the vessel on which my life depended. My spirits at this forsook me, and I expected every moment to go to the bottom; I determined, if I should still be saved, that I would never swear again." (Equiano, 110).

Olaudah was affected in a spiritual way in almost every negative or positive event in his life. He constantly thanked God for his good fortune. "But, I thank God, this fidelity of mine turned out much to my advantage". (Equiano, 90). He even prayed to God in sickness. "I prayed the Lord therefore to spare me". (Equiano, 94). Sometimes he would pray to God submitting a request and then when it was granted he would turn aside from his vow to God. "as I was perfectly restored , and had much business of the vessel to mind, all my endeavors to keep up my integrity, and perform my promise to God, began to fail". (Equiano, 94). He futher states, "Alas! How prone is the heart to leave that God it wishes to love!" (Equiano, 94). Even when Olaudah was depressed and even contemplated suicide he found comfort in his Christian friends and what he perceived to be the word of God. "He prayed for me, and I believe that he prevailed on my behalf, as my burden was then greatly removed, and I found a heart-felt resignation to the will of God." (Equiano, 143). By the end of the book Olaudah

has been baptized and indoctrinated with the gospel of the Christians. He no longer practiced

the rites of the Jews, or the other practices that he spoke about that he observed from his

childhood. But, he was in essence a full-fledge European slave trader who participated in the

enslavement of his own people and other Africans. Although at times he had a guilty

conscience, somehow he felt like to live like a good old boy was the will of God.

Many leaders in the black community are just like Olaudah Equiano or Gustavas Vassa.

They feel like they are doing the will of God just because they are diligent in studying their

slave master's religion (Christianity), get up and go to work every day, and tell the world that

they're all about peace, all the while they are key figures in promoting and continuing human

slavery and death. Gustava Vassa was not the only one of his kind, on the contrary, almost

every single leader African Americans have had have taken up the proverb of Gustava Vassa,

which is one of the principle reasons African Americans are the "tail and not the head", the

borrower and not the lender, and the consumer and not the producer. Almost every African

American leader that attempts to better the conditions of their black communities does so by

the doctrines and guidance of white America or the Europeans. When was the last time an

African leader stood up and said , "If you want your oppression to end then turn back to the

ways of your forefathers Abraham, Isaac, and Jacob. Return to the way of the right ruling,

those who obeyed the laws of the Creator that created all living things." Who, among the Af-

rican-American community is interested in restoring the kingdom of Yahudah and the old kingdom of Israel that was ruled by King David and his son King Solomon? Until a leader like this rises up there will be many Gustava Vassas leading their people into the pit.

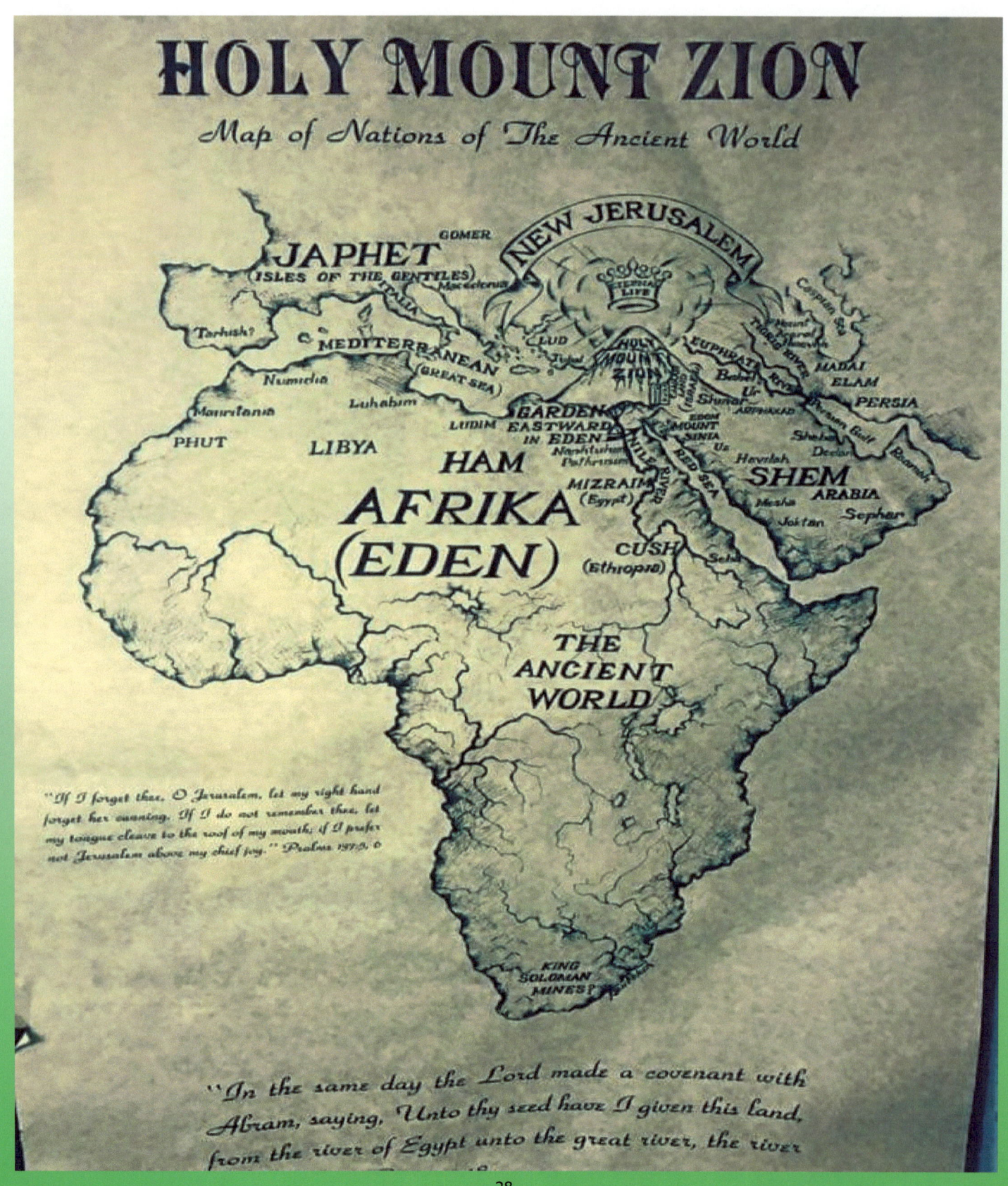

Ruakh of the Fist

Nuba Bujutsu

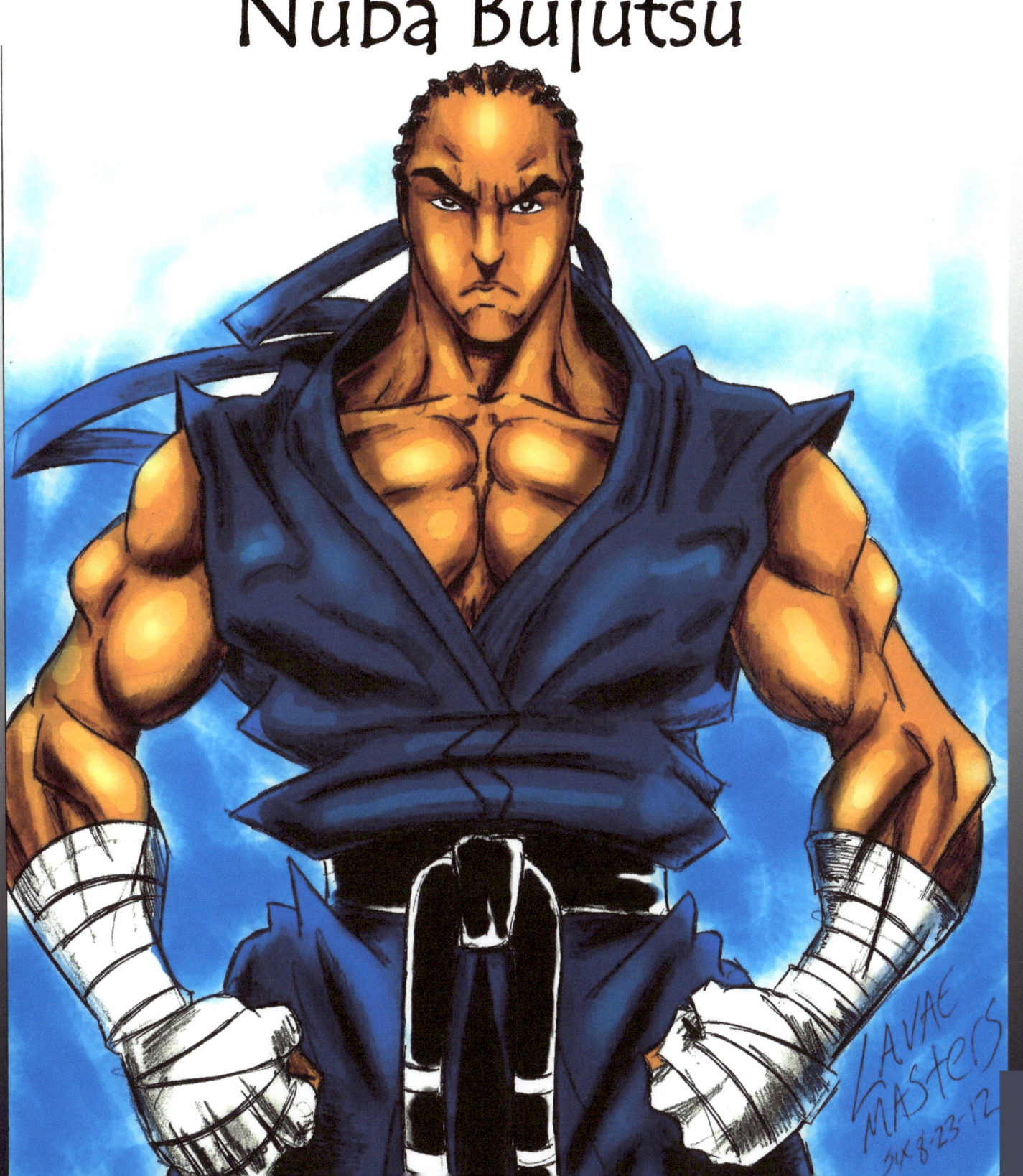

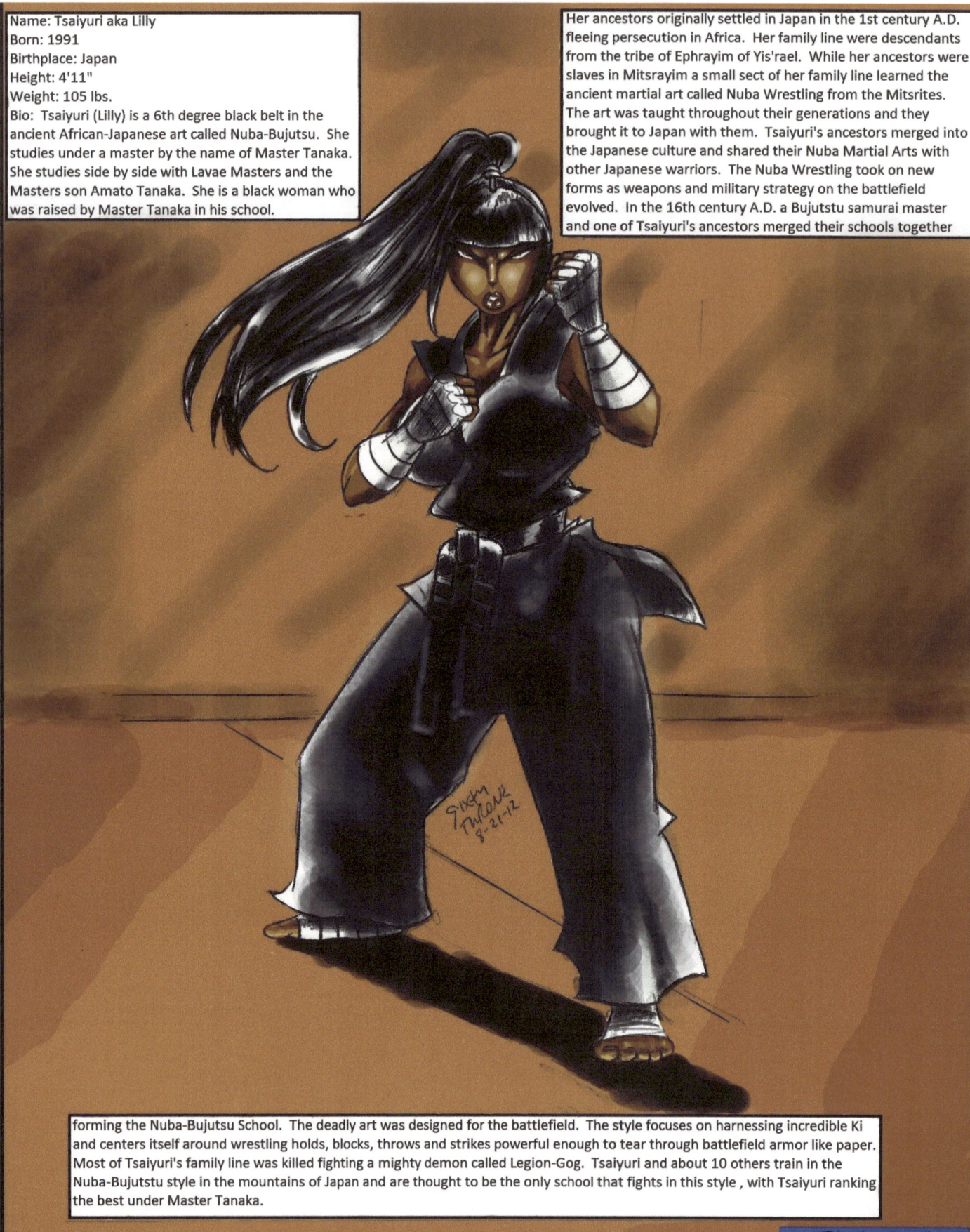

Name: Tsaiyuri aka Lilly
Born: 1991
Birthplace: Japan
Height: 4'11"
Weight: 105 lbs.
Bio: Tsaiyuri (Lilly) is a 6th degree black belt in the ancient African-Japanese art called Nuba-Bujutsu. She studies under a master by the name of Master Tanaka. She studies side by side with Lavae Masters and the Masters son Amato Tanaka. She is a black woman who was raised by Master Tanaka in his school.

Her ancestors originally settled in Japan in the 1st century A.D. fleeing persecution in Africa. Her family line were descendants from the tribe of Ephrayim of Yis'rael. While her ancestors were slaves in Mitsrayim a small sect of her family line learned the ancient martial art called Nuba Wrestling from the Mitsrites. The art was taught throughout their generations and they brought it to Japan with them. Tsaiyuri's ancestors merged into the Japanese culture and shared their Nuba Martial Arts with other Japanese warriors. The Nuba Wrestling took on new forms as weapons and military strategy on the battlefield evolved. In the 16th century A.D. a Bujutstu samurai master and one of Tsaiyuri's ancestors merged their schools together

forming the Nuba-Bujutsu School. The deadly art was designed for the battlefield. The style focuses on harnessing incredible Ki and centers itself around wrestling holds, blocks, throws and strikes powerful enough to tear through battlefield armor like paper. Most of Tsaiyuri's family line was killed fighting a mighty demon called Legion-Gog. Tsaiyuri and about 10 others train in the Nuba-Bujutstu style in the mountains of Japan and are thought to be the only school that fights in this style , with Tsaiyuri ranking the best under Master Tanaka.

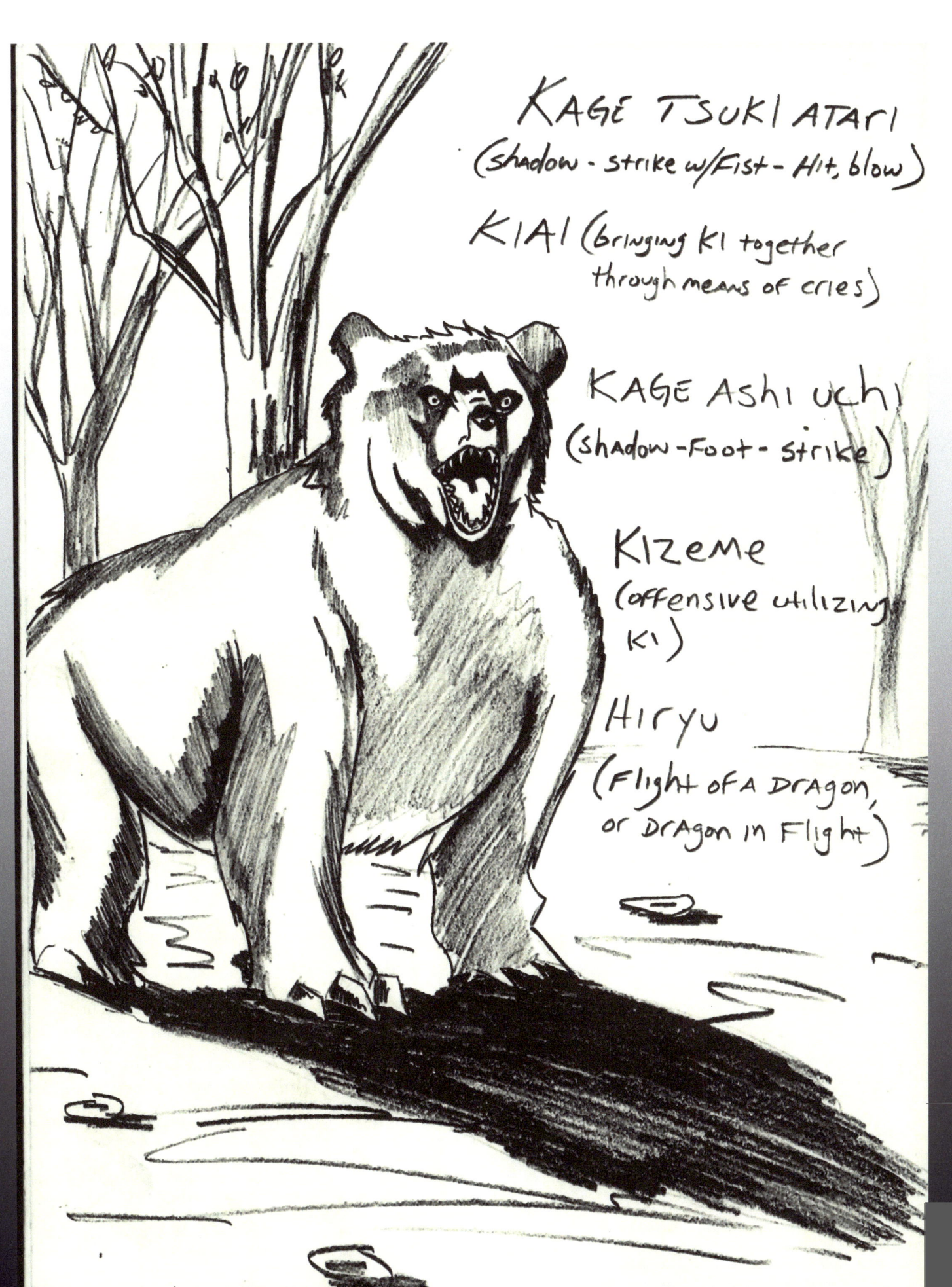

KAGE TSUKI ATARI
(shadow - strike w/Fist - Hit, blow)

KIAI (bringing KI together
through means of cries)

KAGE ASHI UCHI
(shadow - Foot - strike)

KIZEME
(offensive utilizing
KI)

Hiryu
(Flight of a Dragon,
or Dragon in Flight)

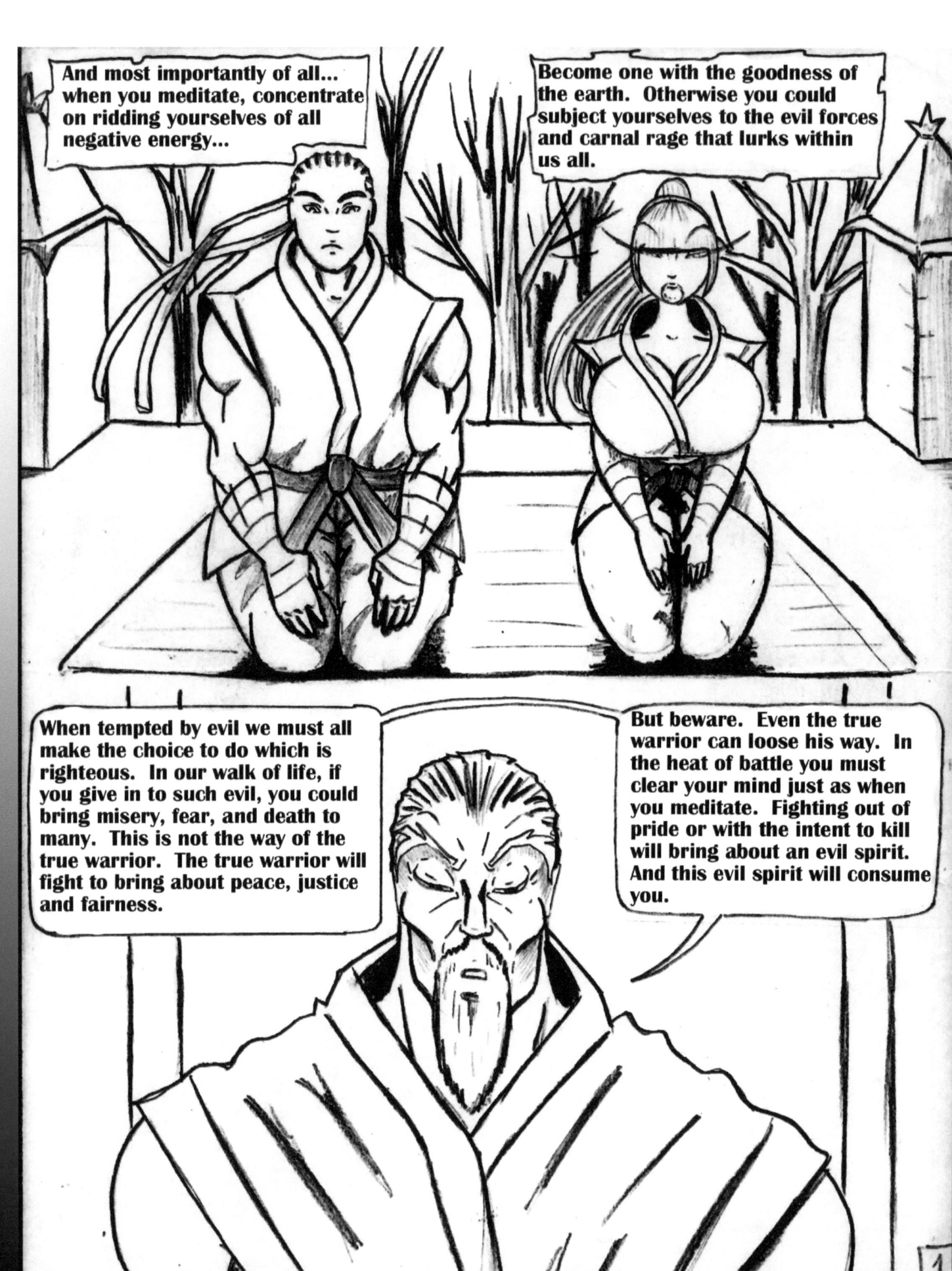

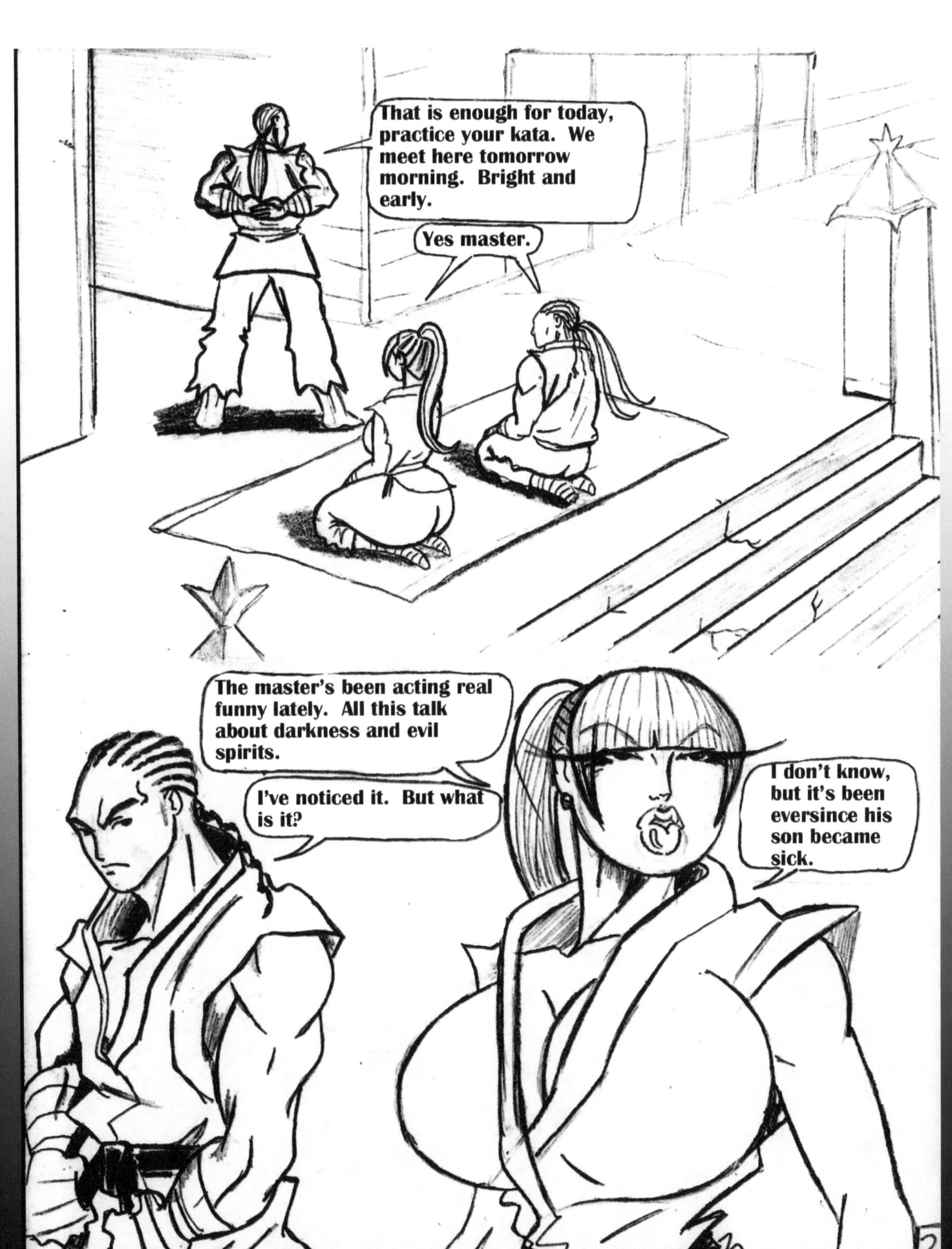

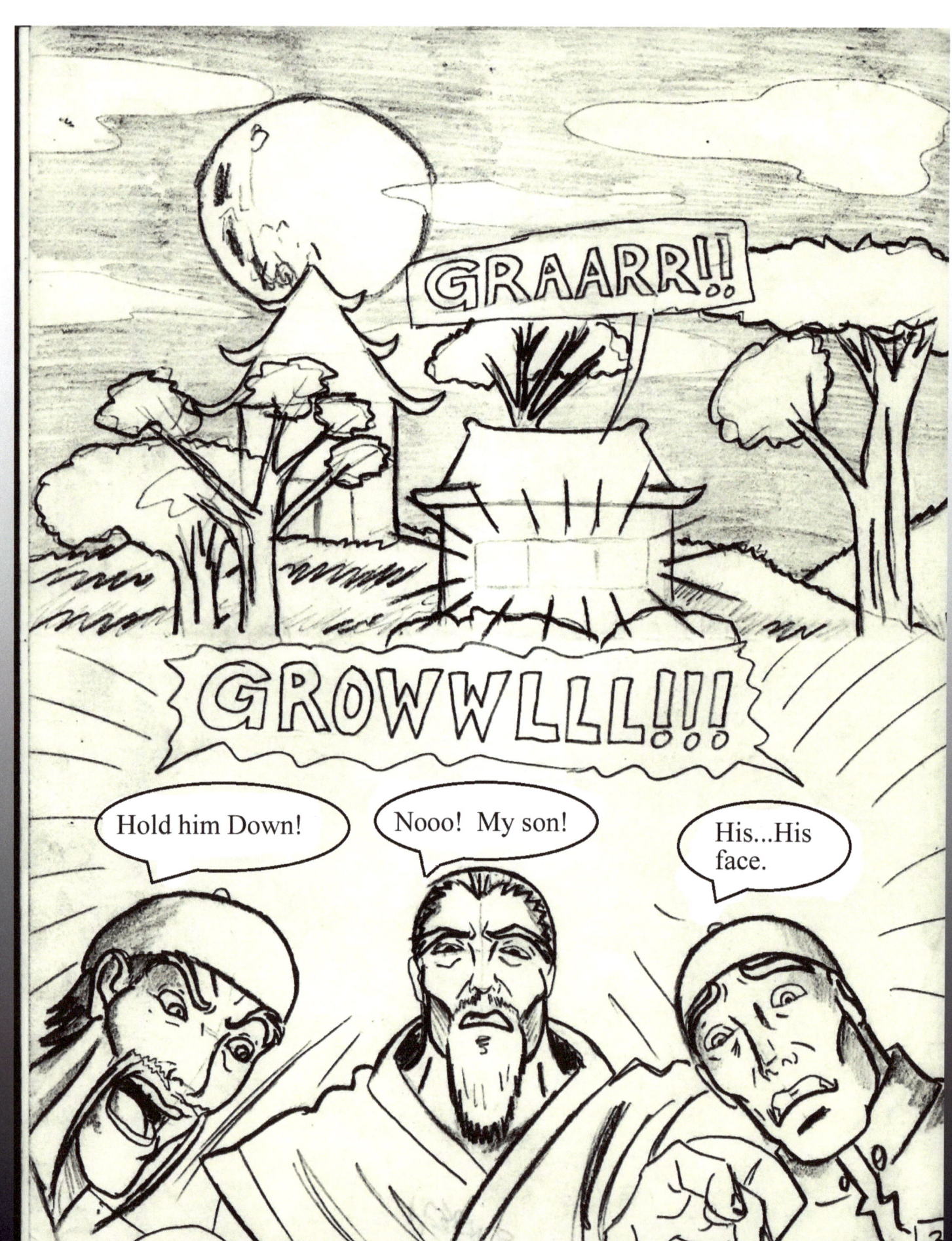

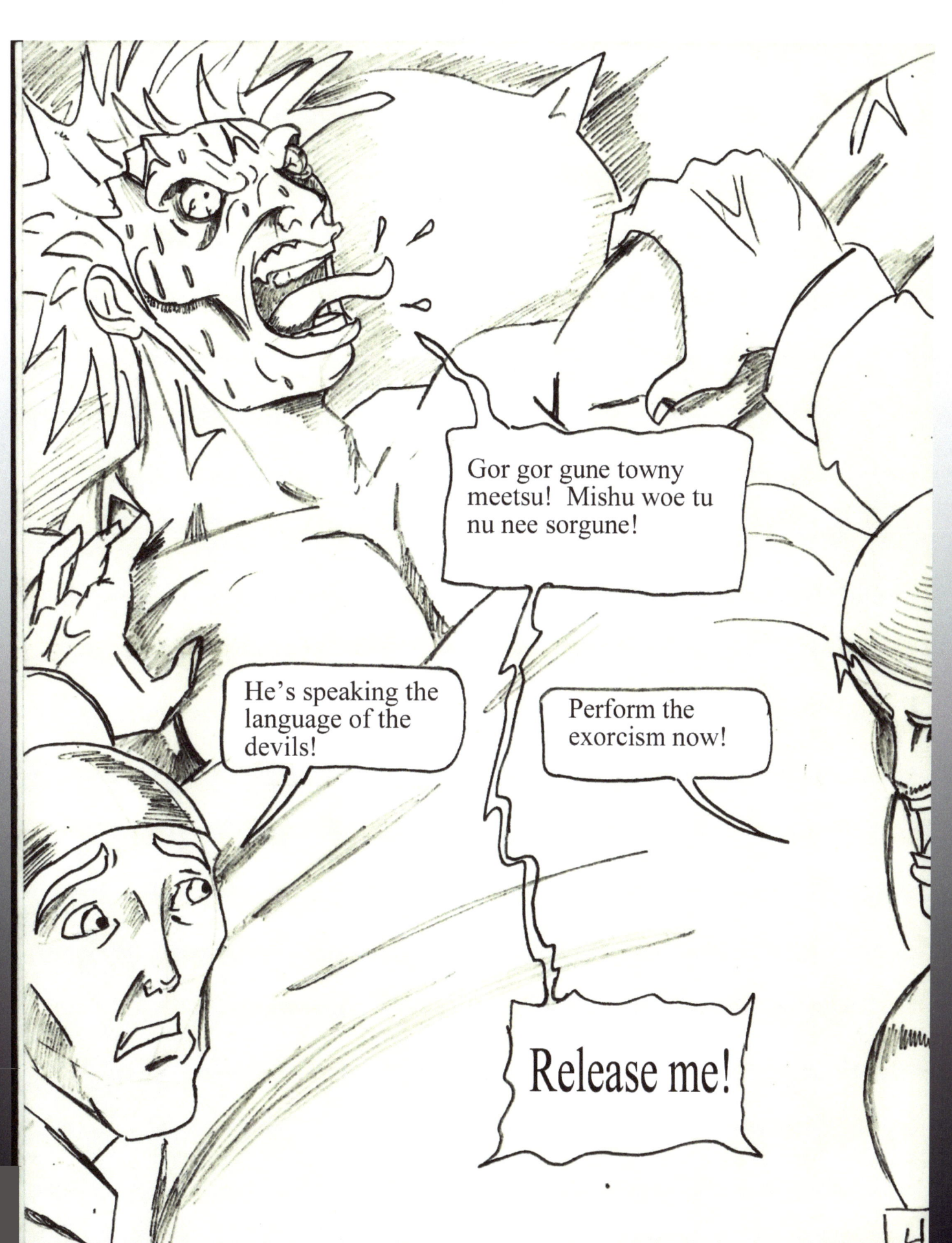

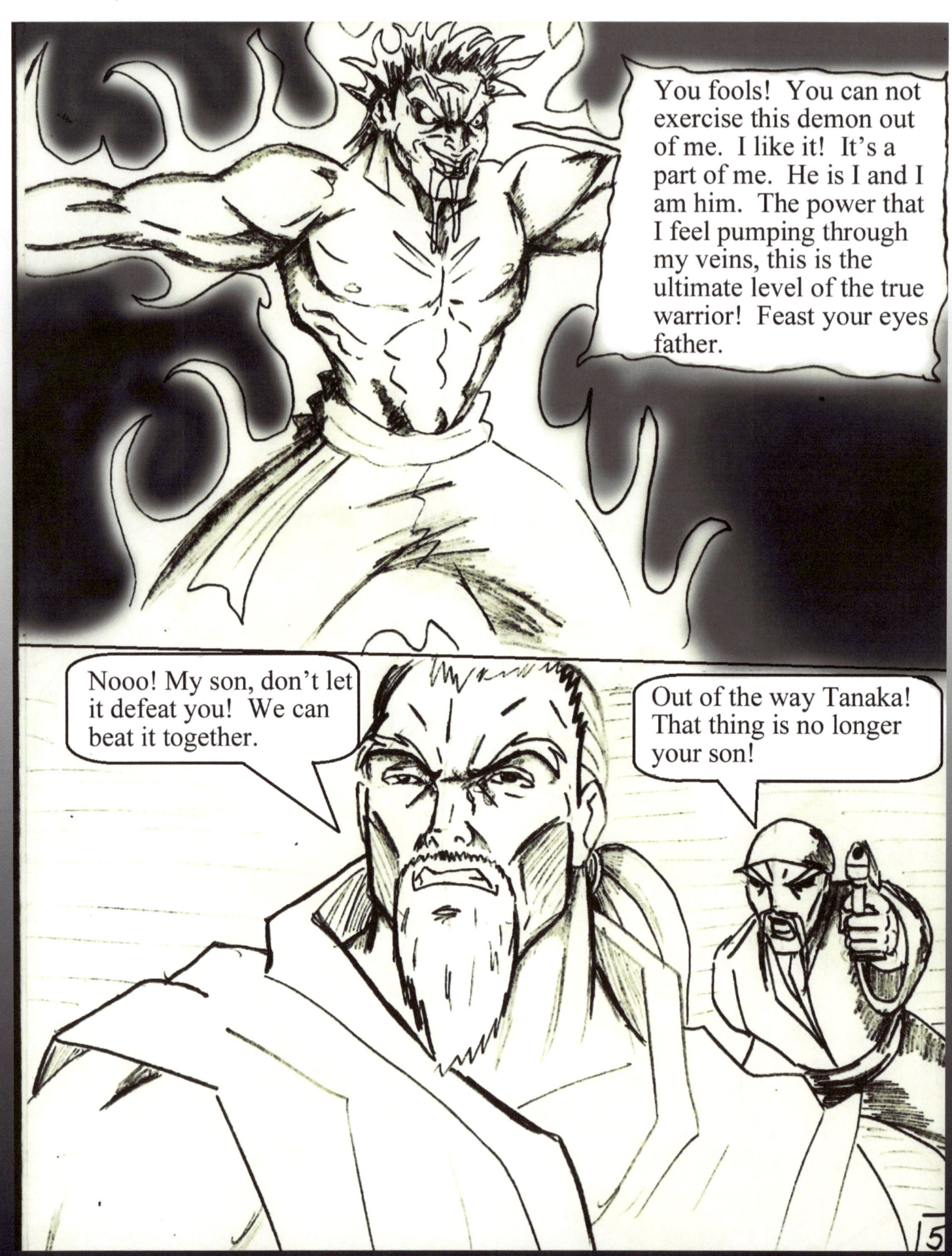

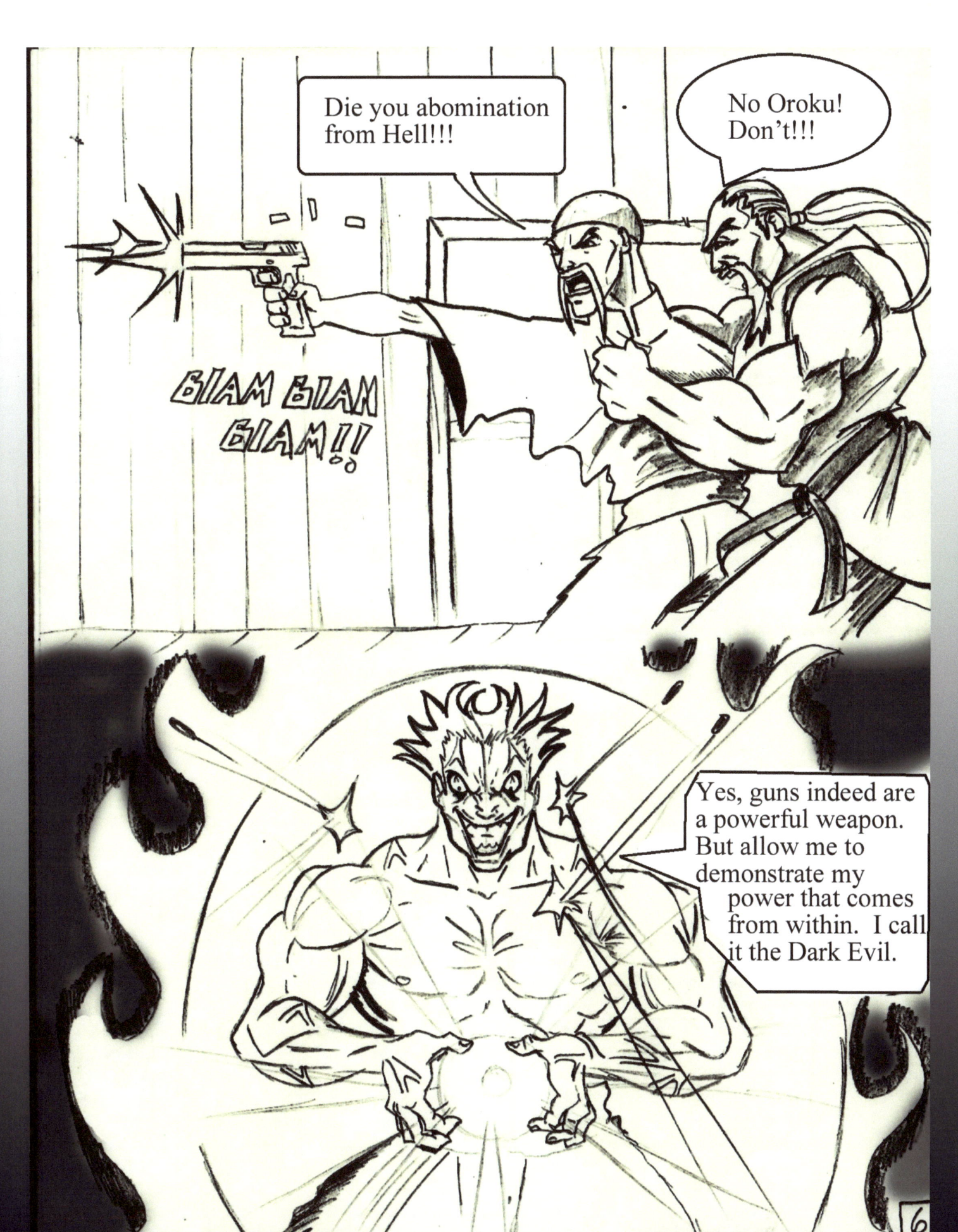

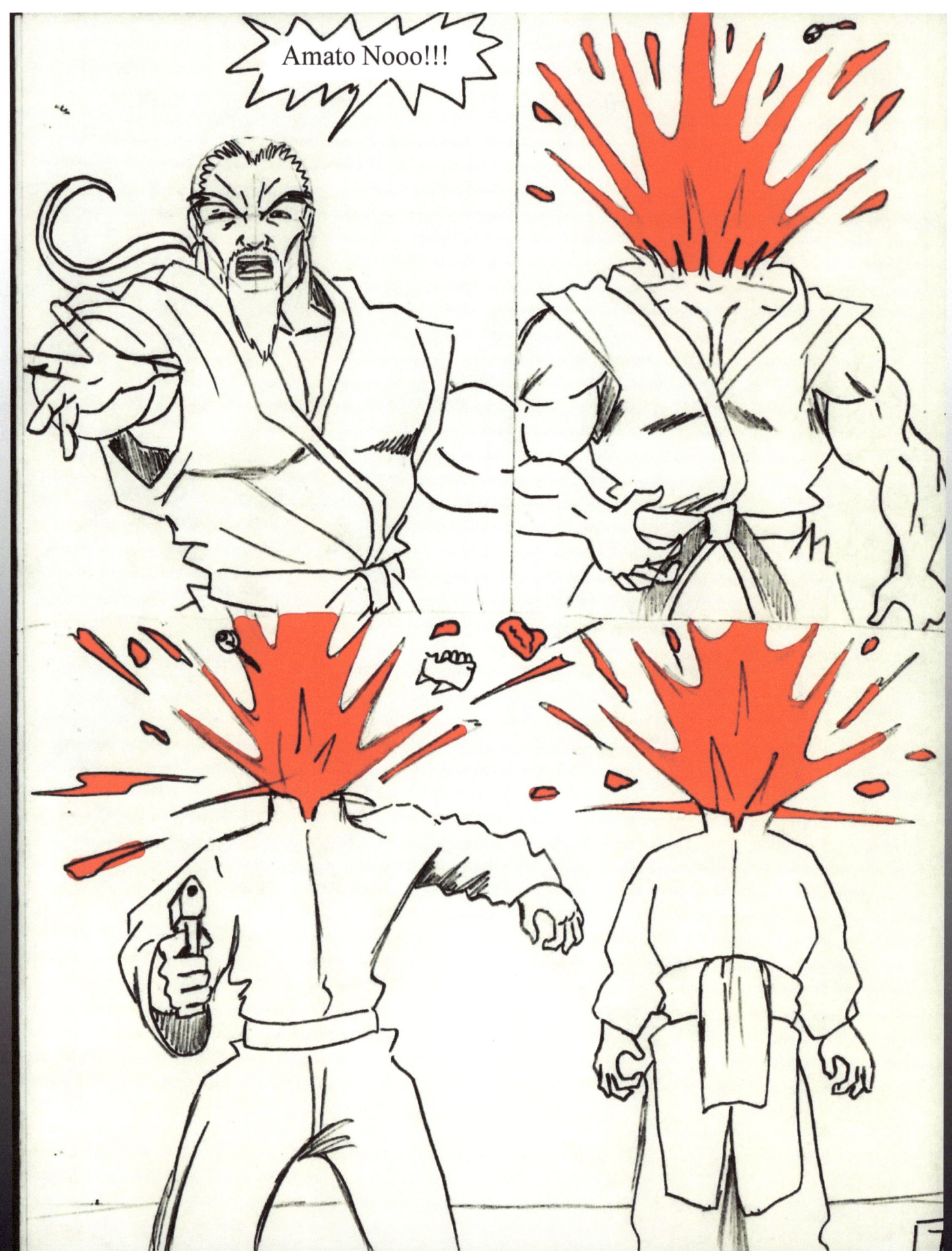

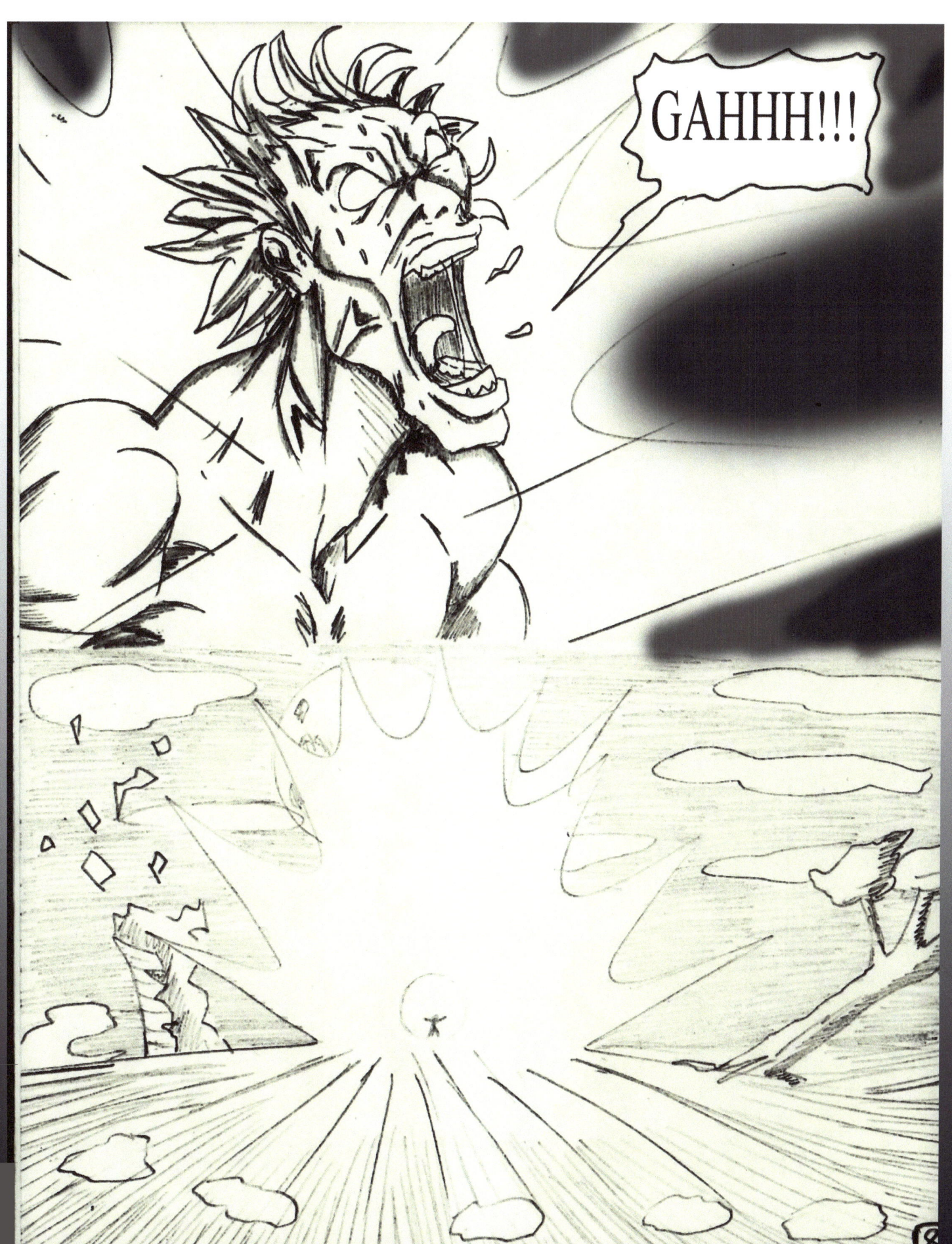

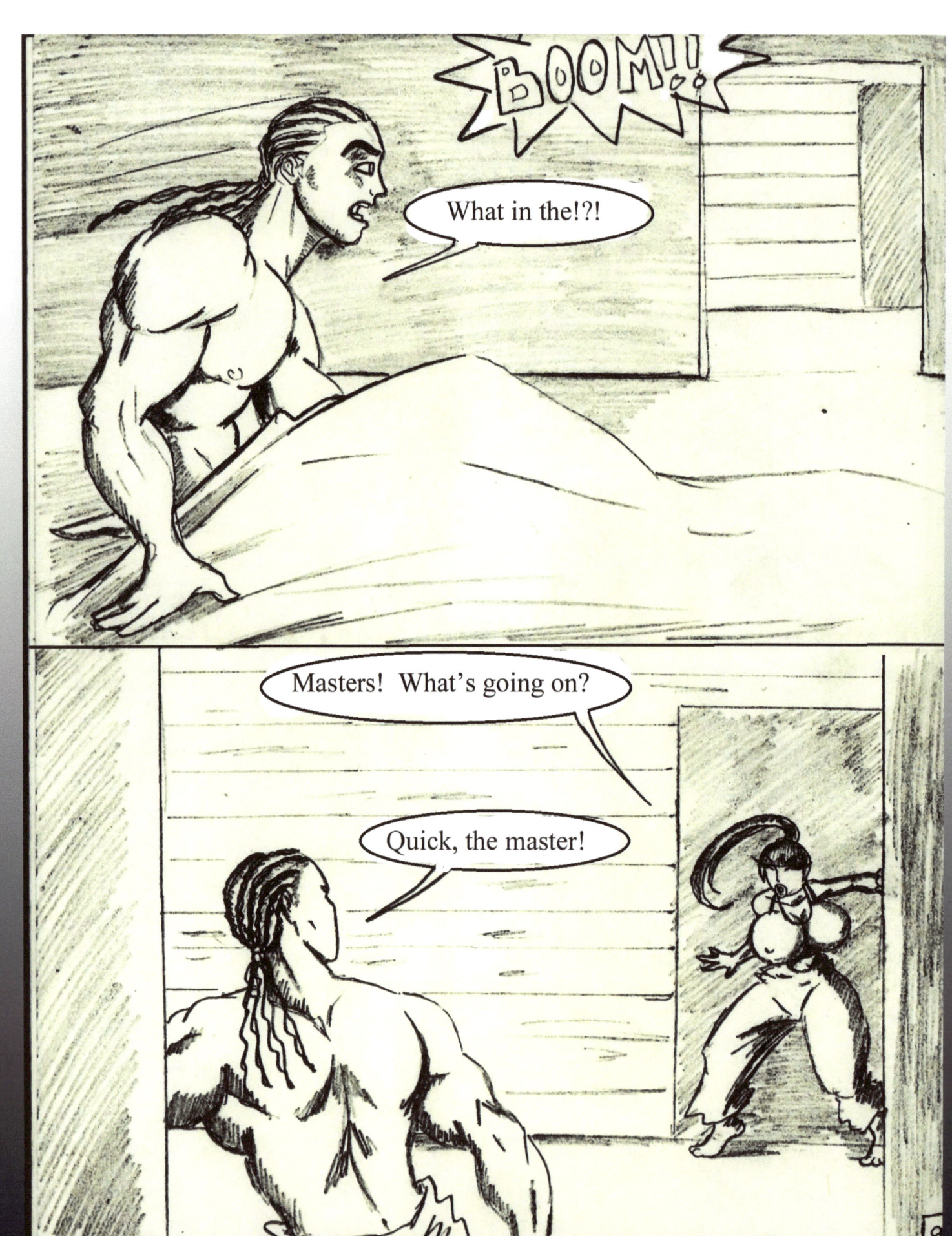

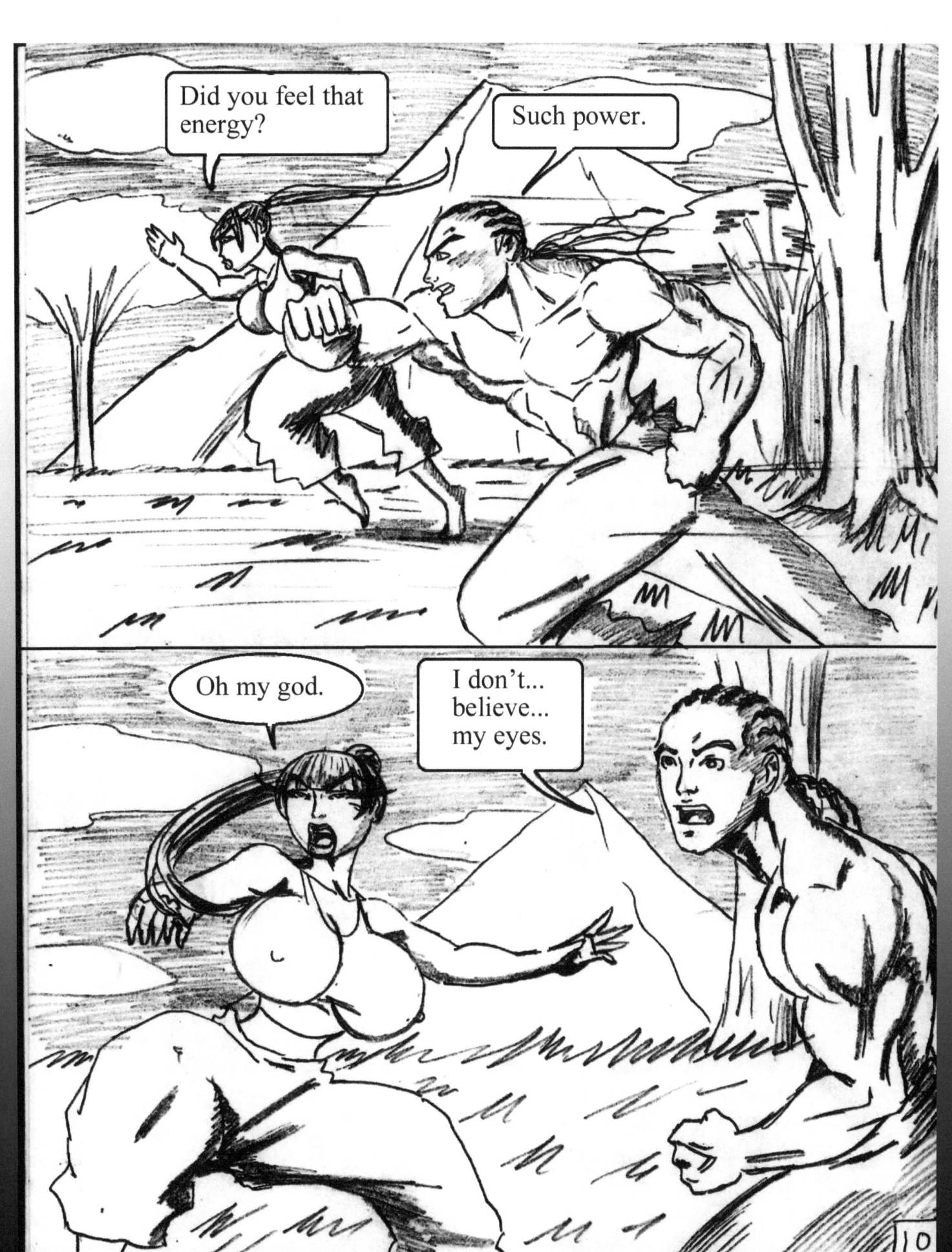

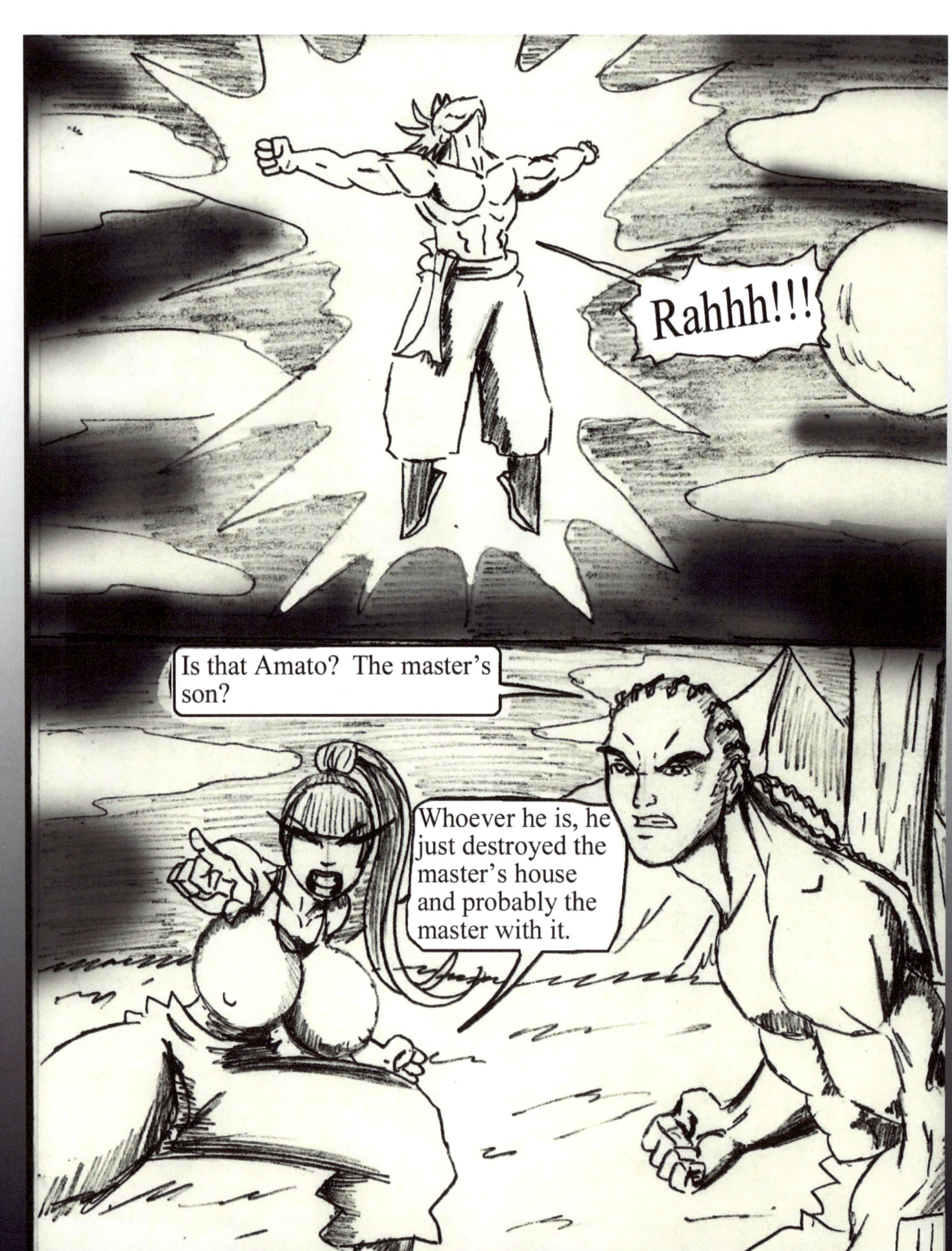

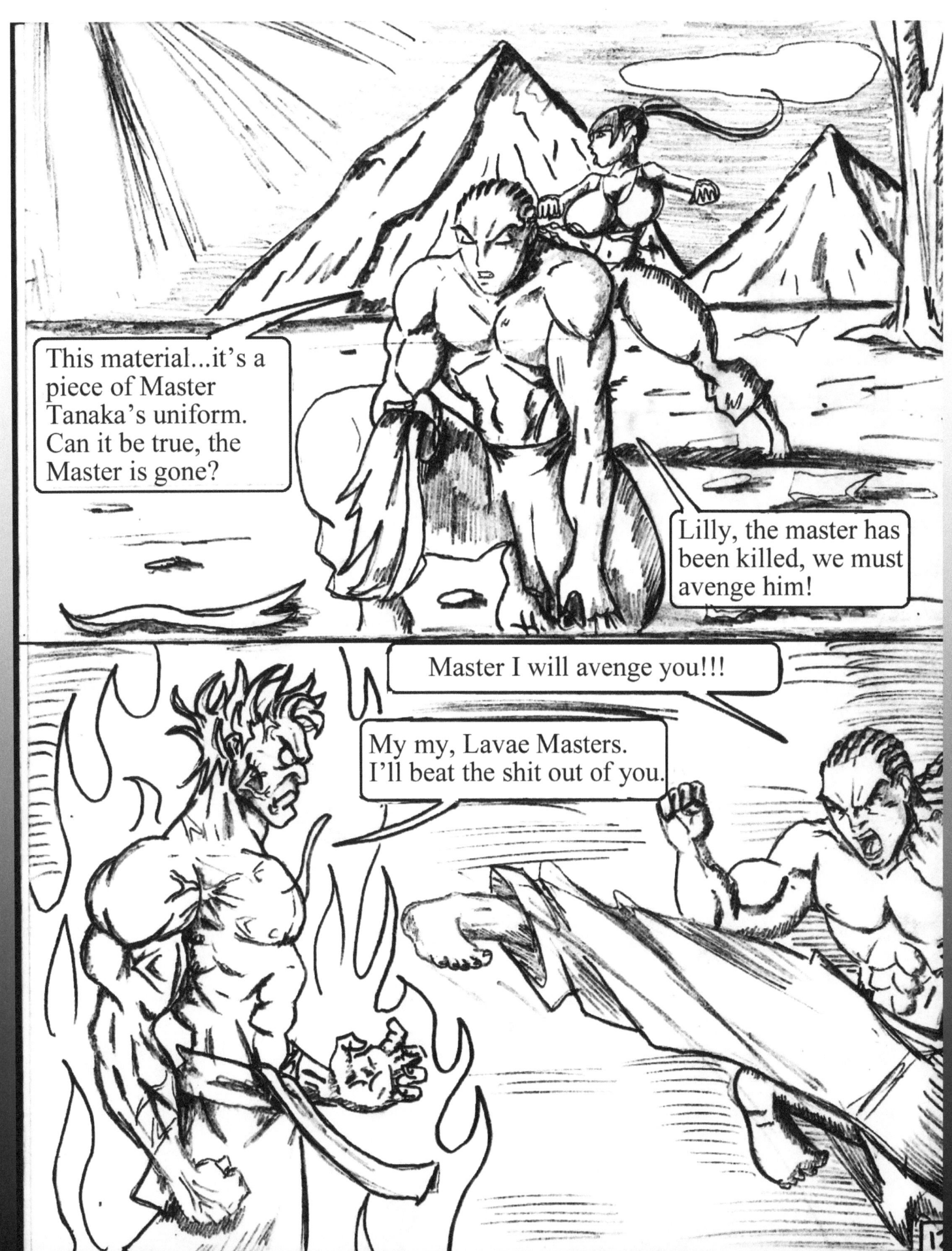

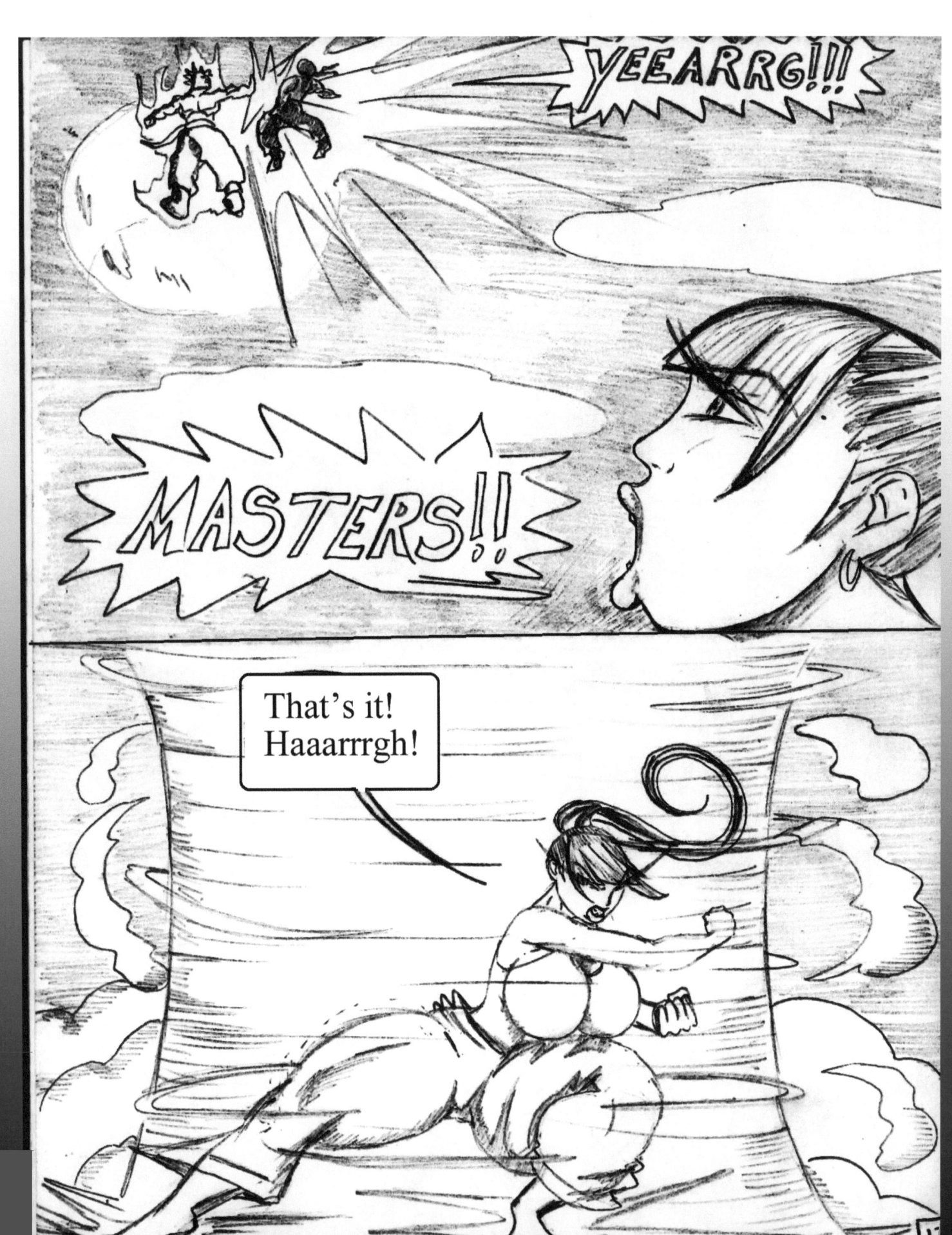

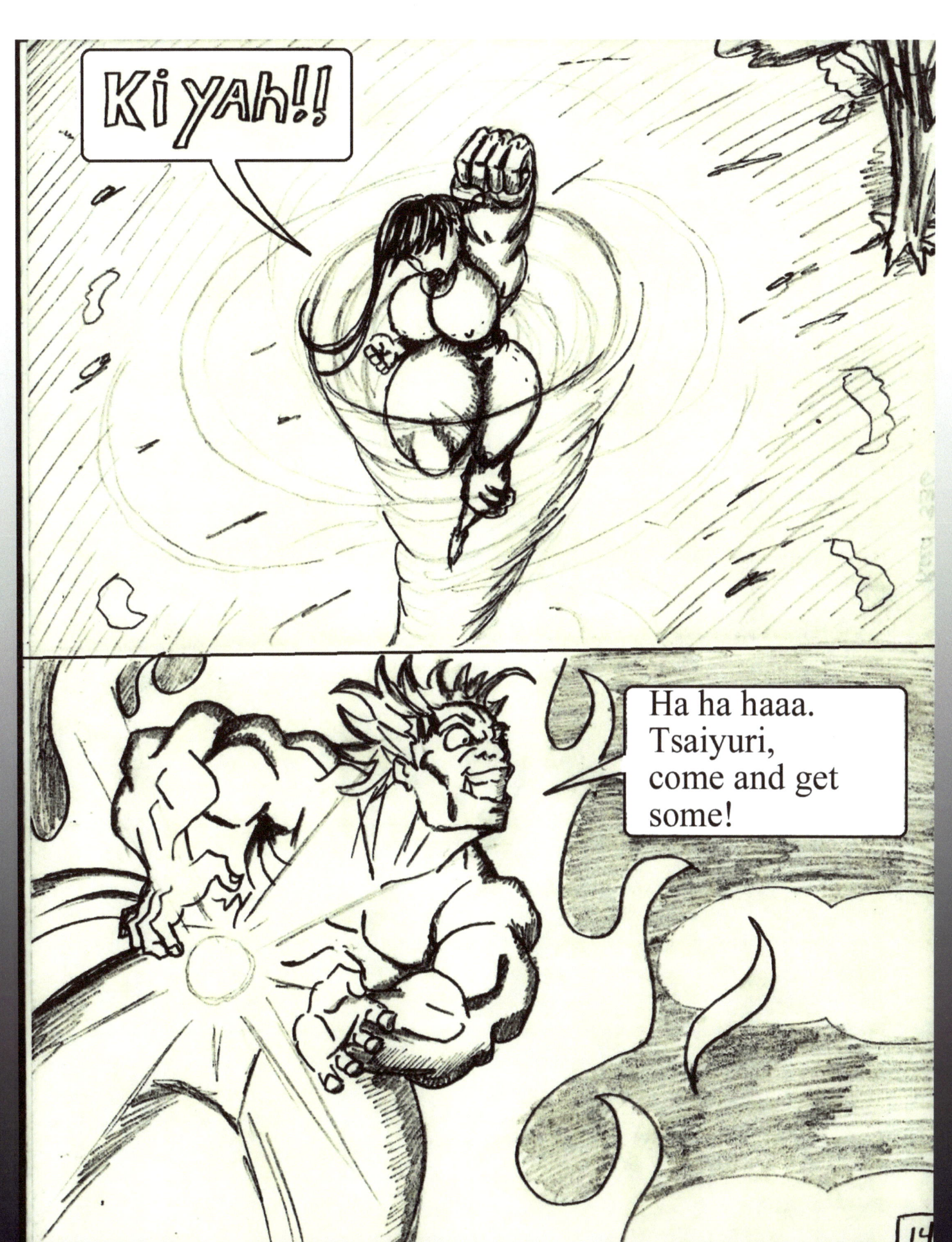

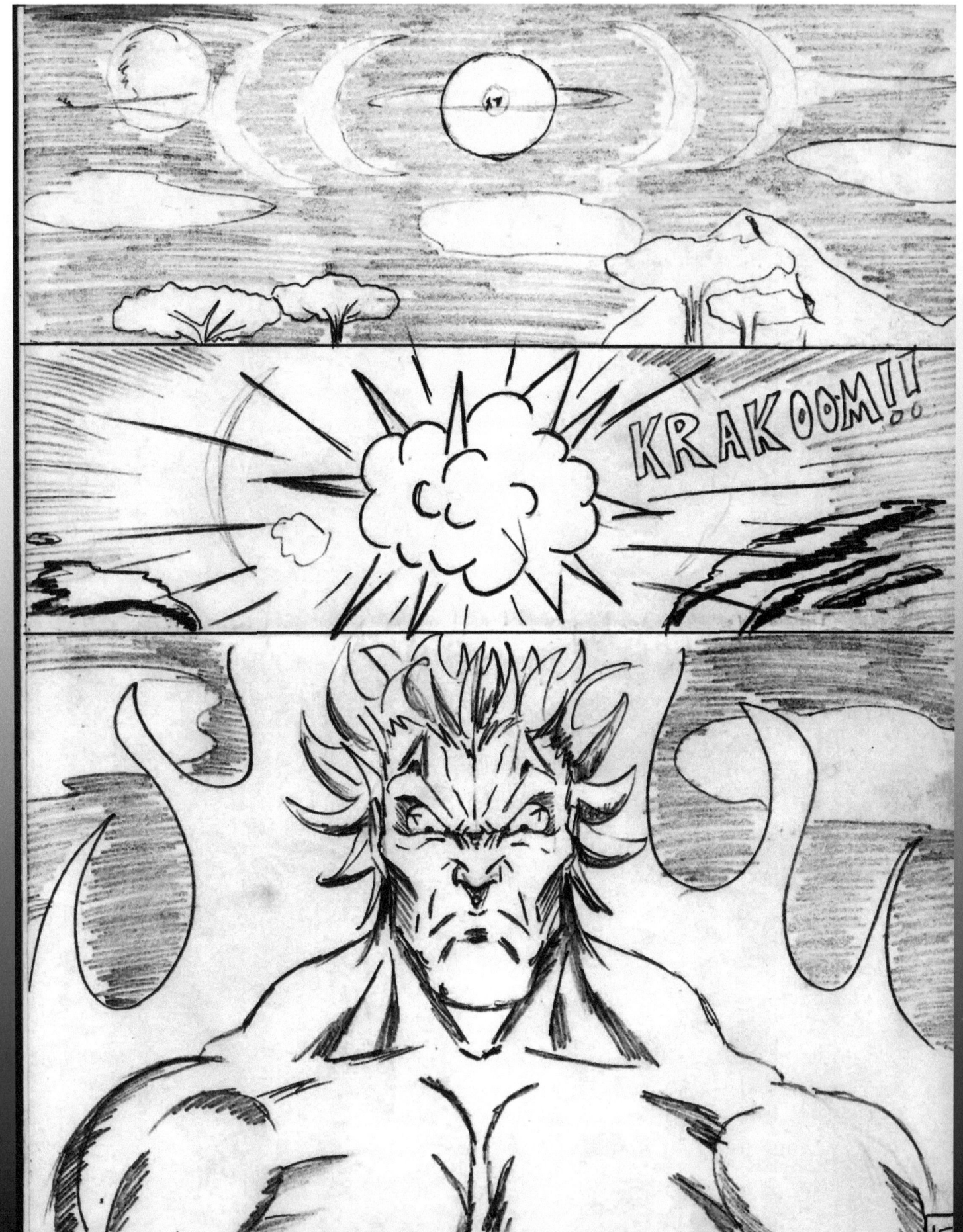

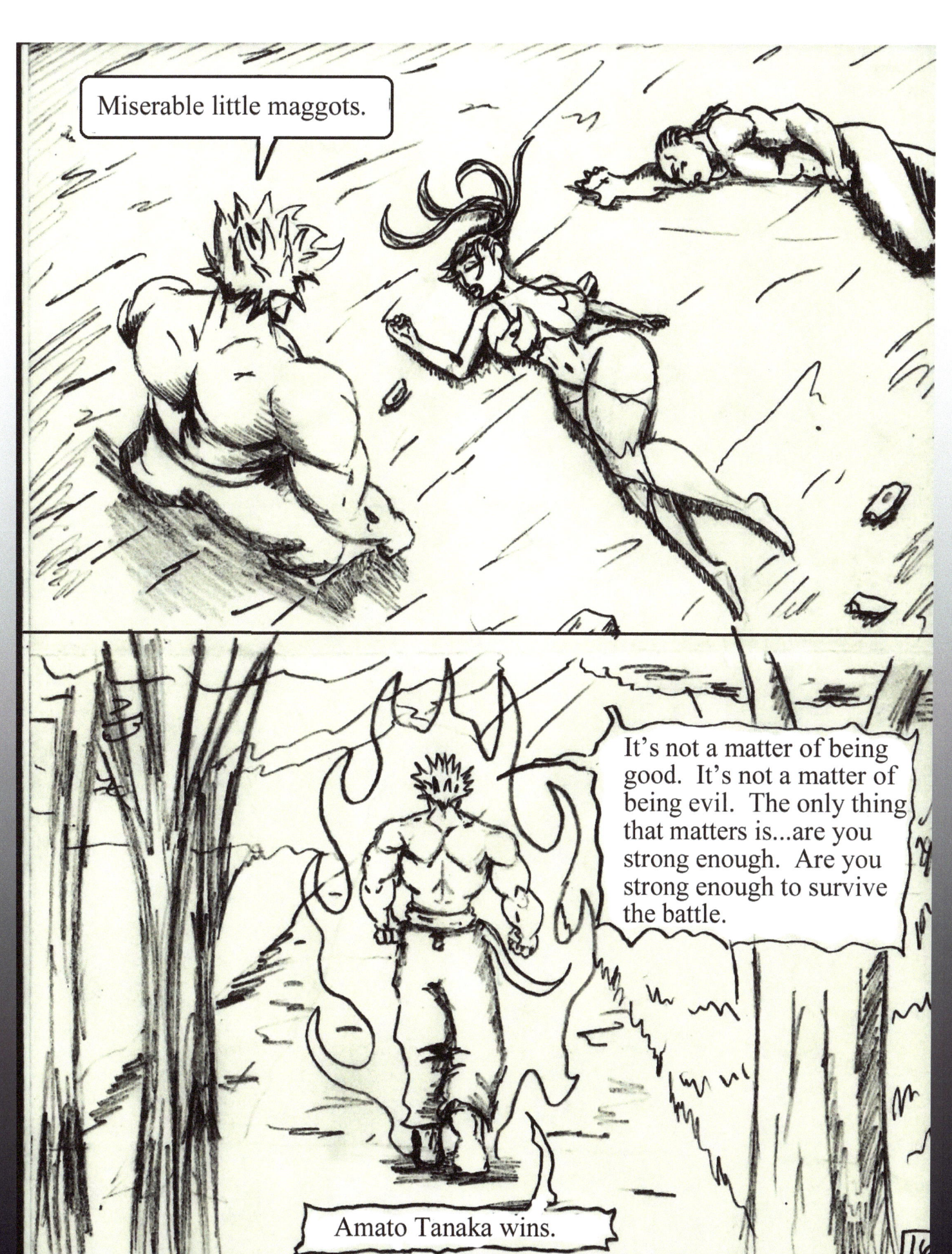

Art Gallery

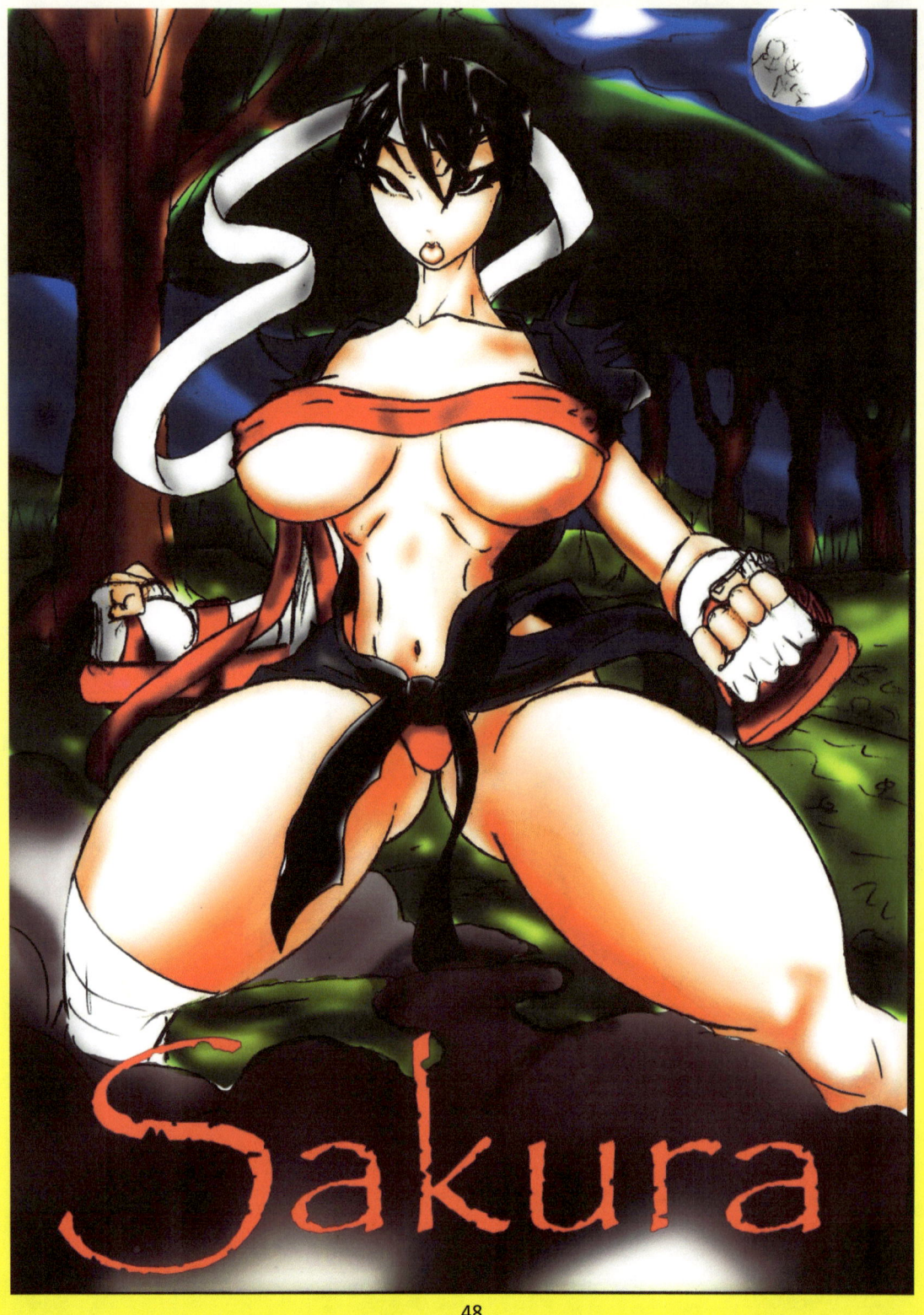

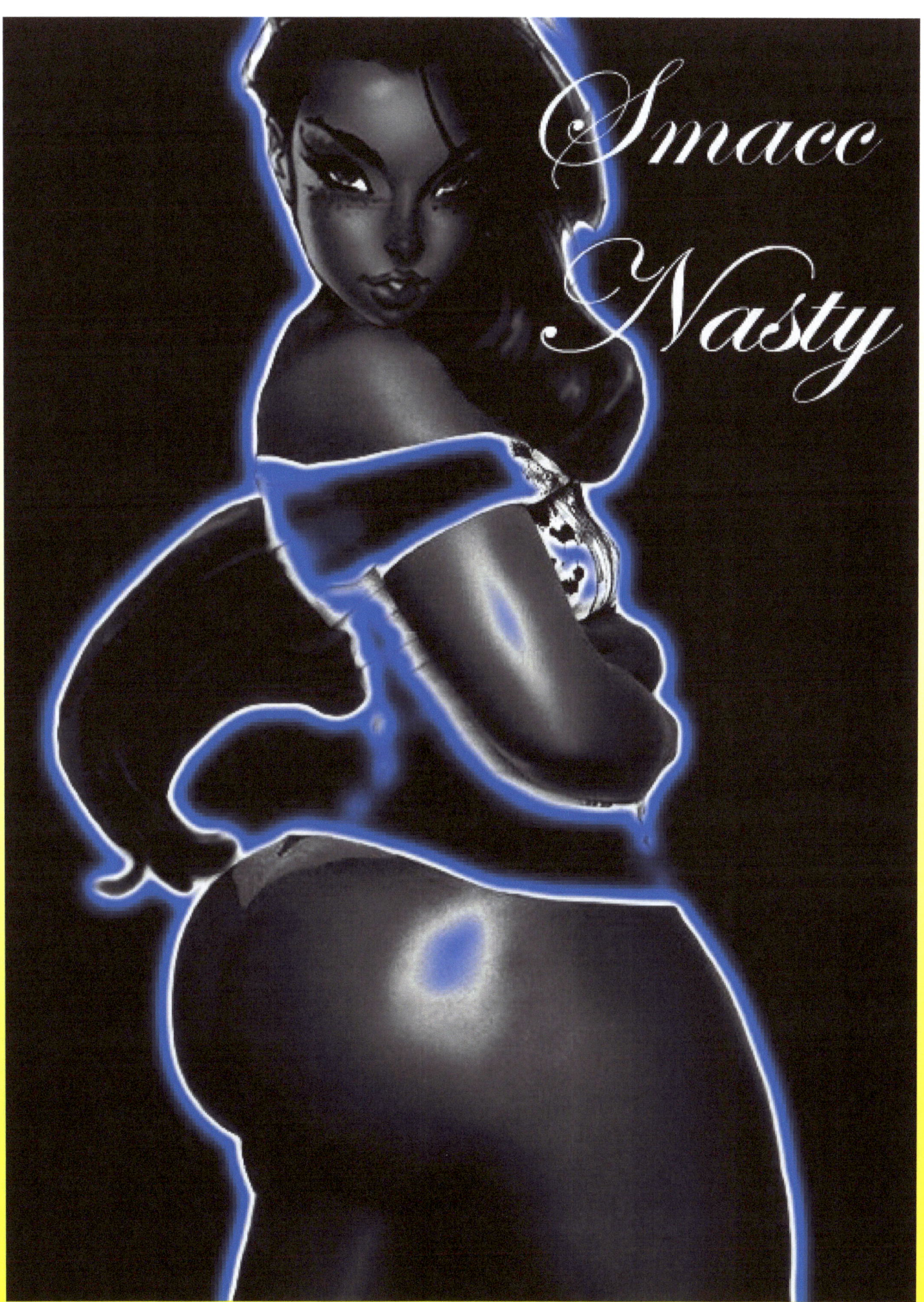

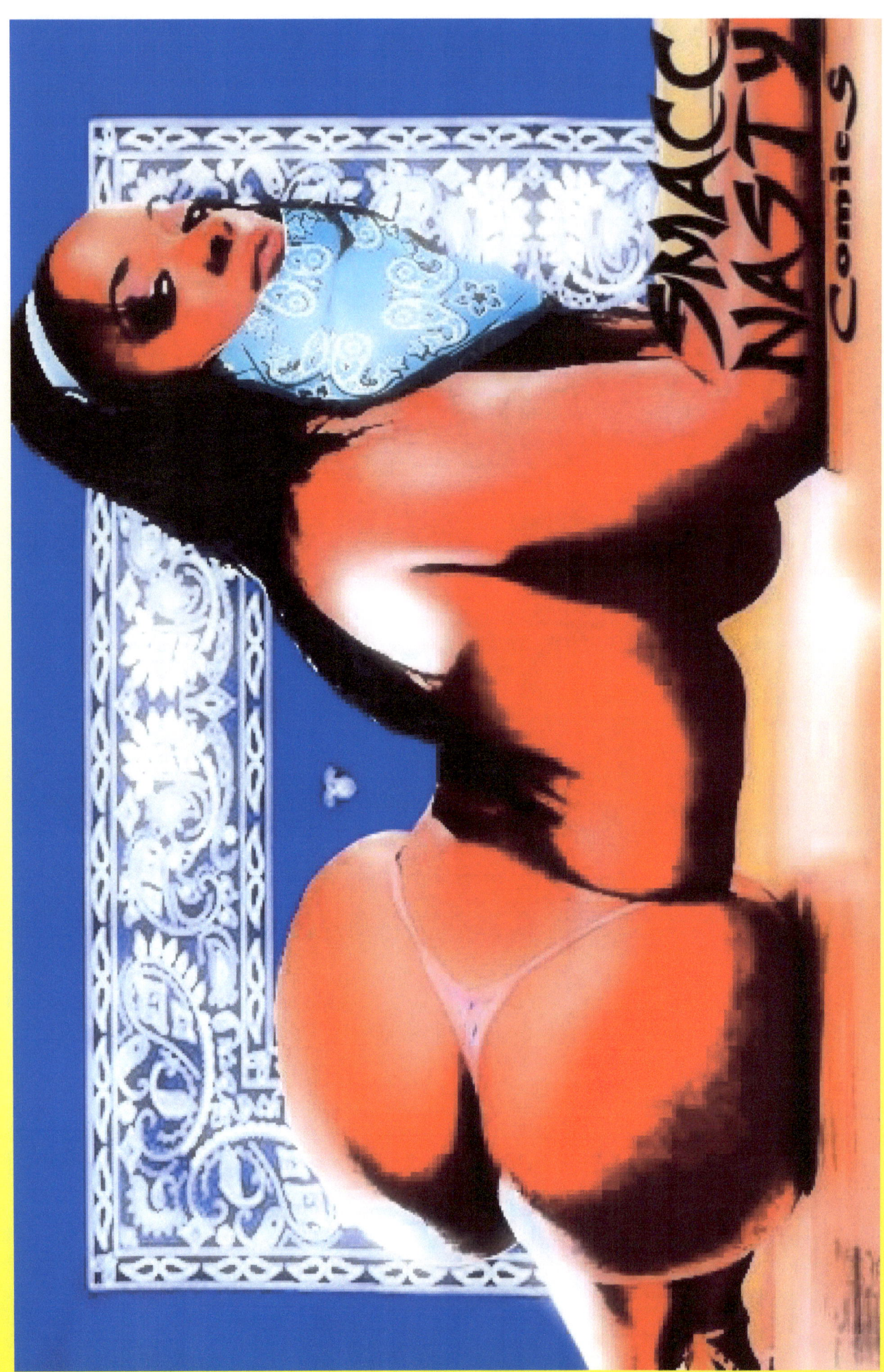

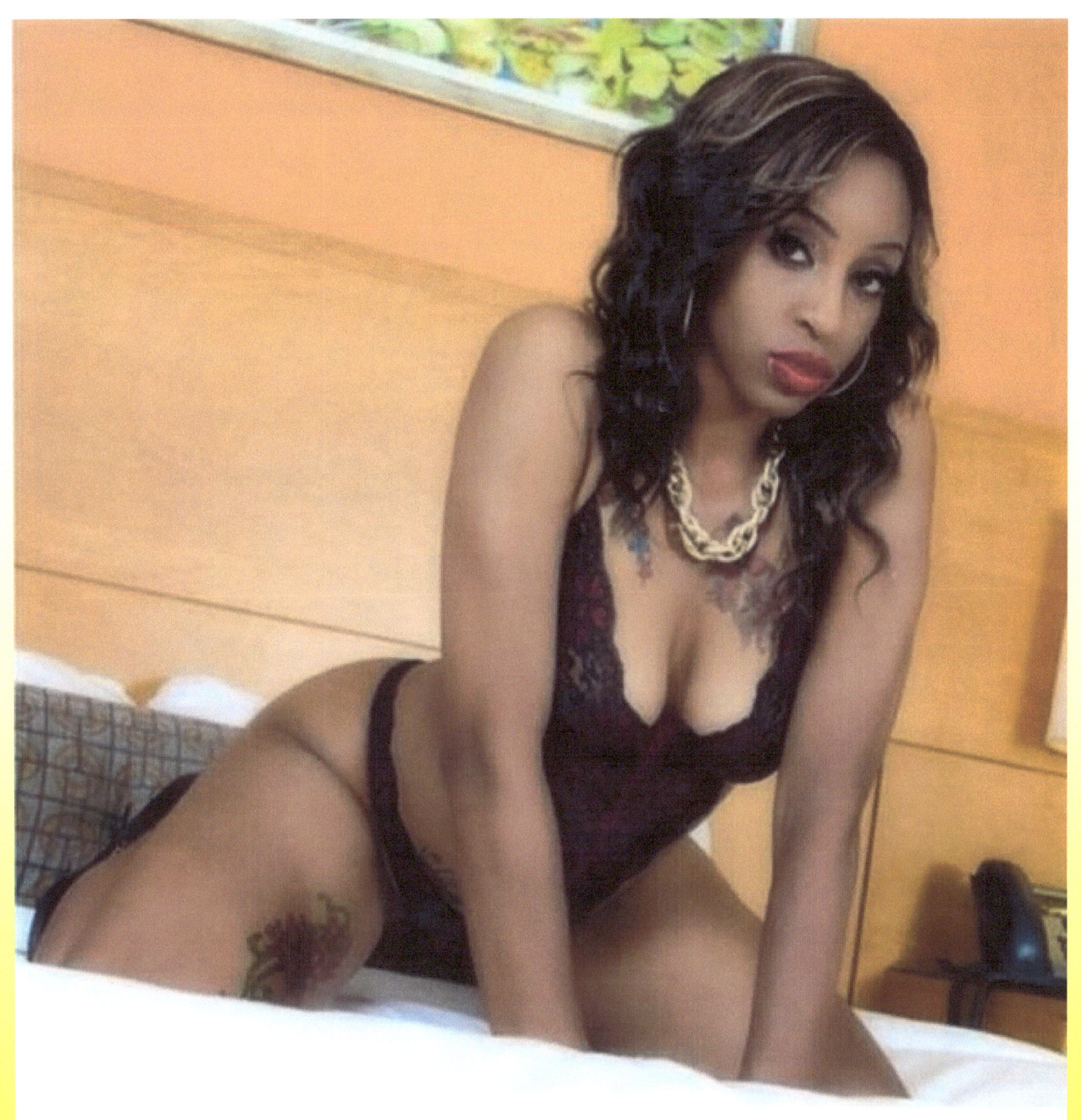

Model: Amber Atkins

Contact info: newelegendz@gmail.com,

 David Bristol, Manager

Photoagraphy by Fyne Girlz

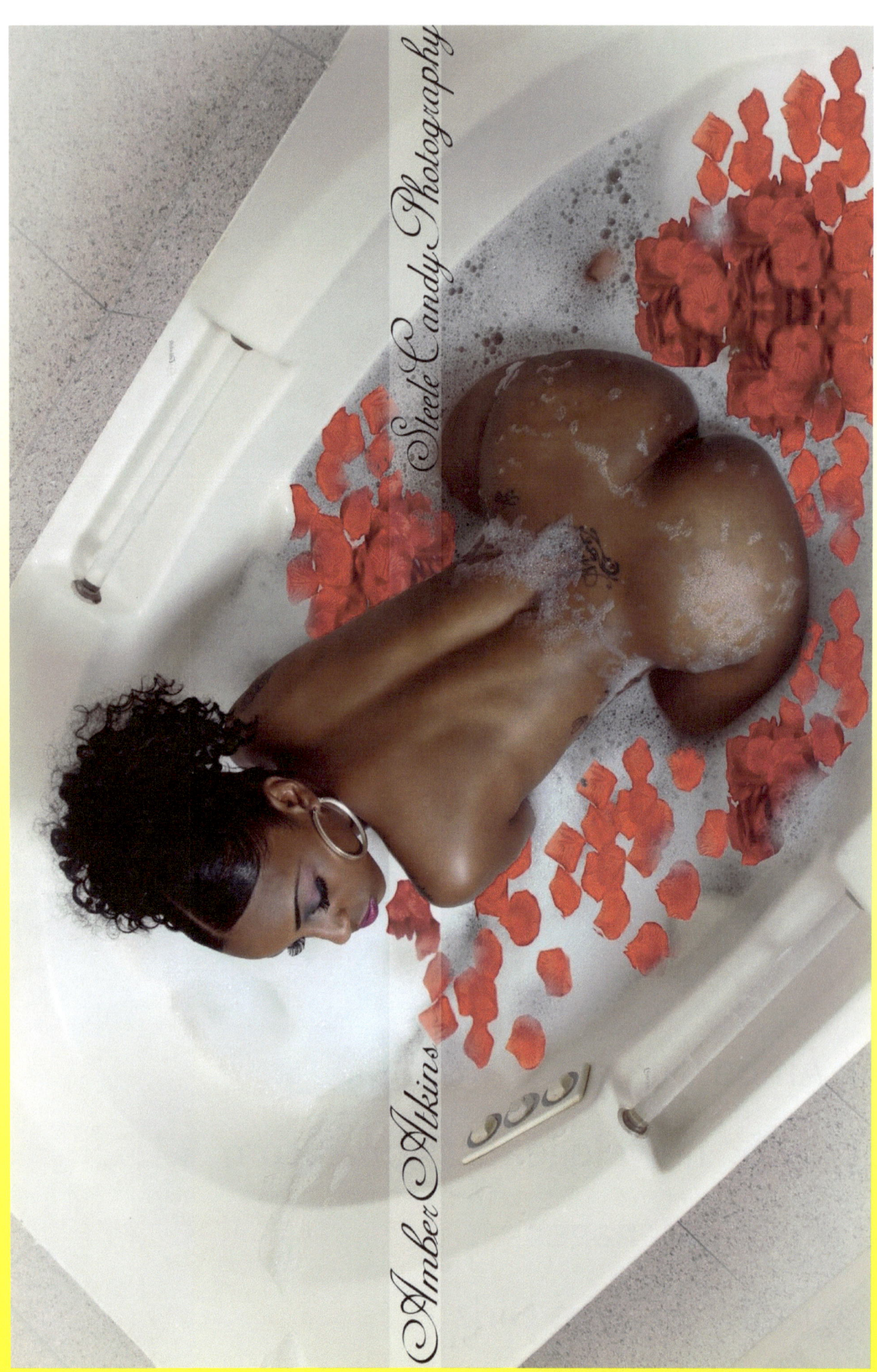

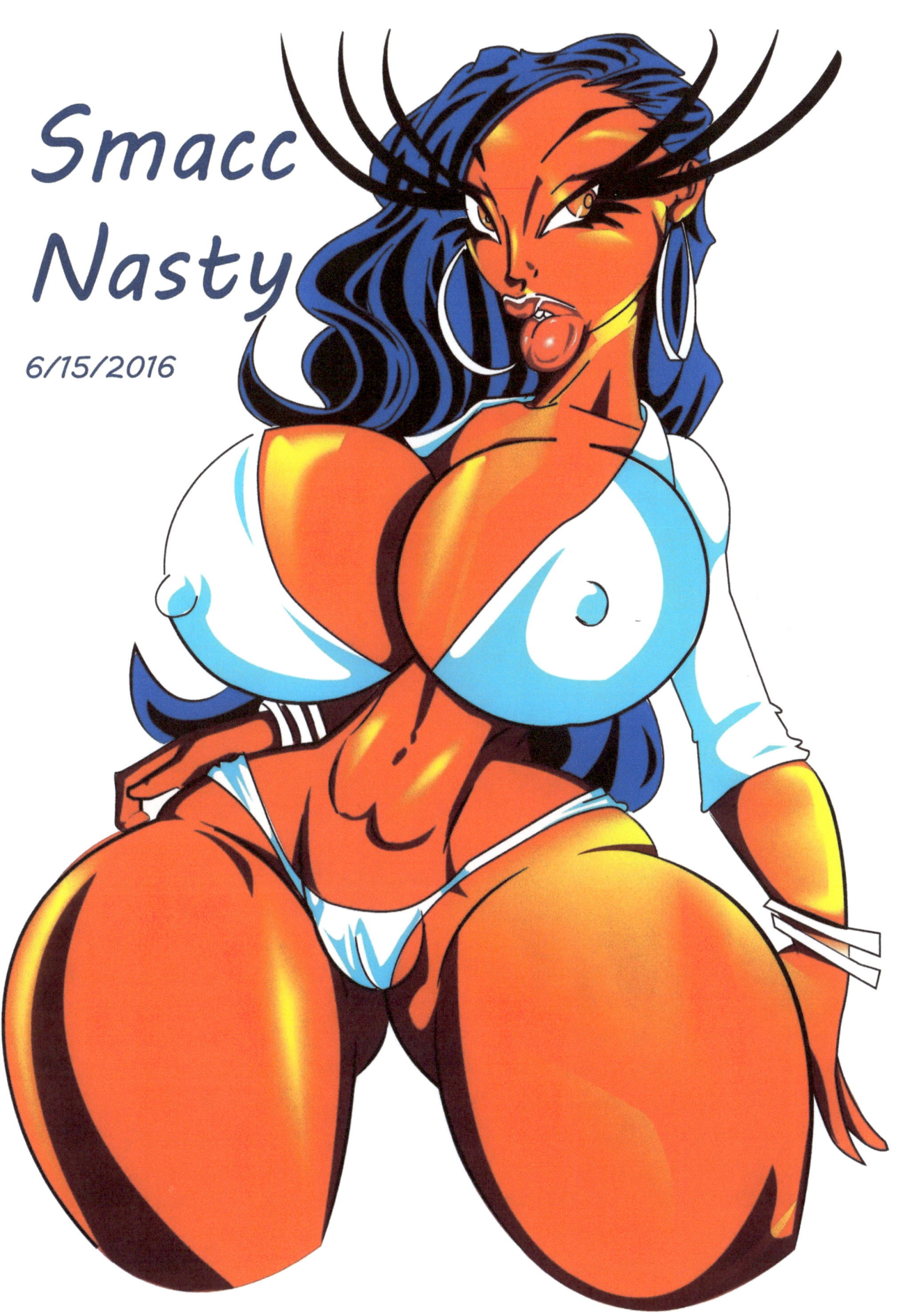

Smacc
Nasty

6/15/2016

The CEO

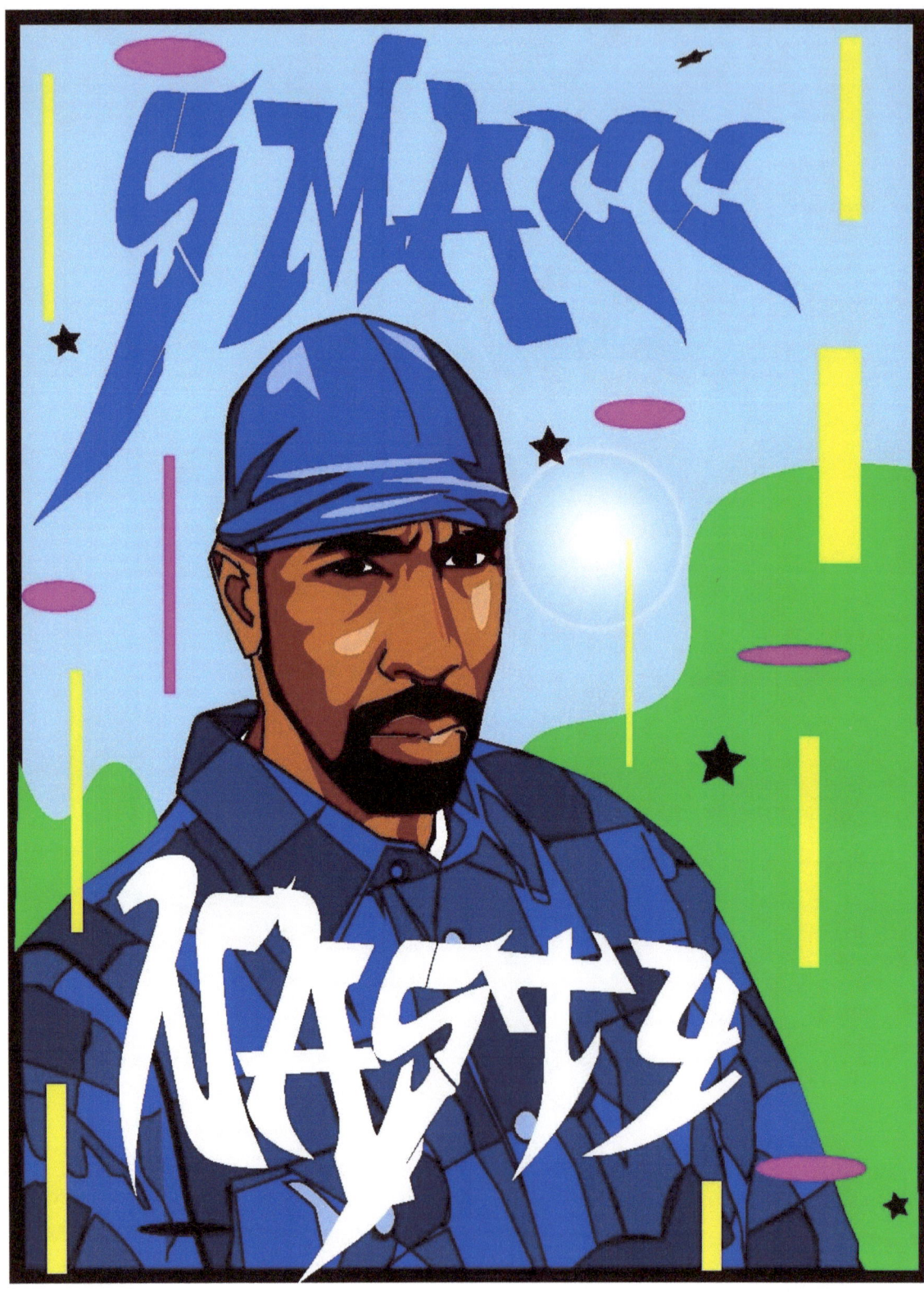

VIOLENCE HAS GREAT CONSEQUENCES

COMING SOON! A SMACC NASTY GRAPHIC NOVEL

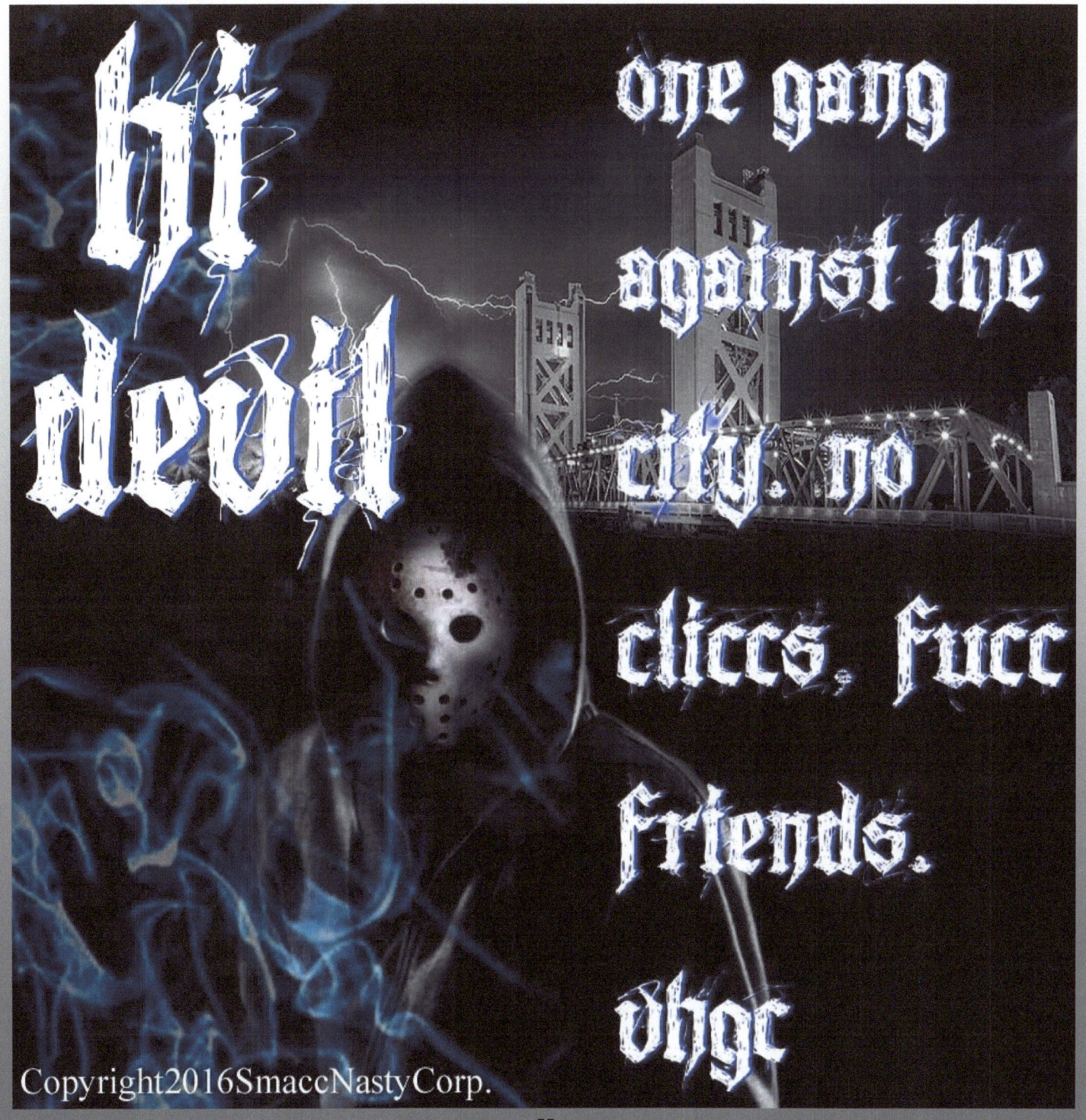

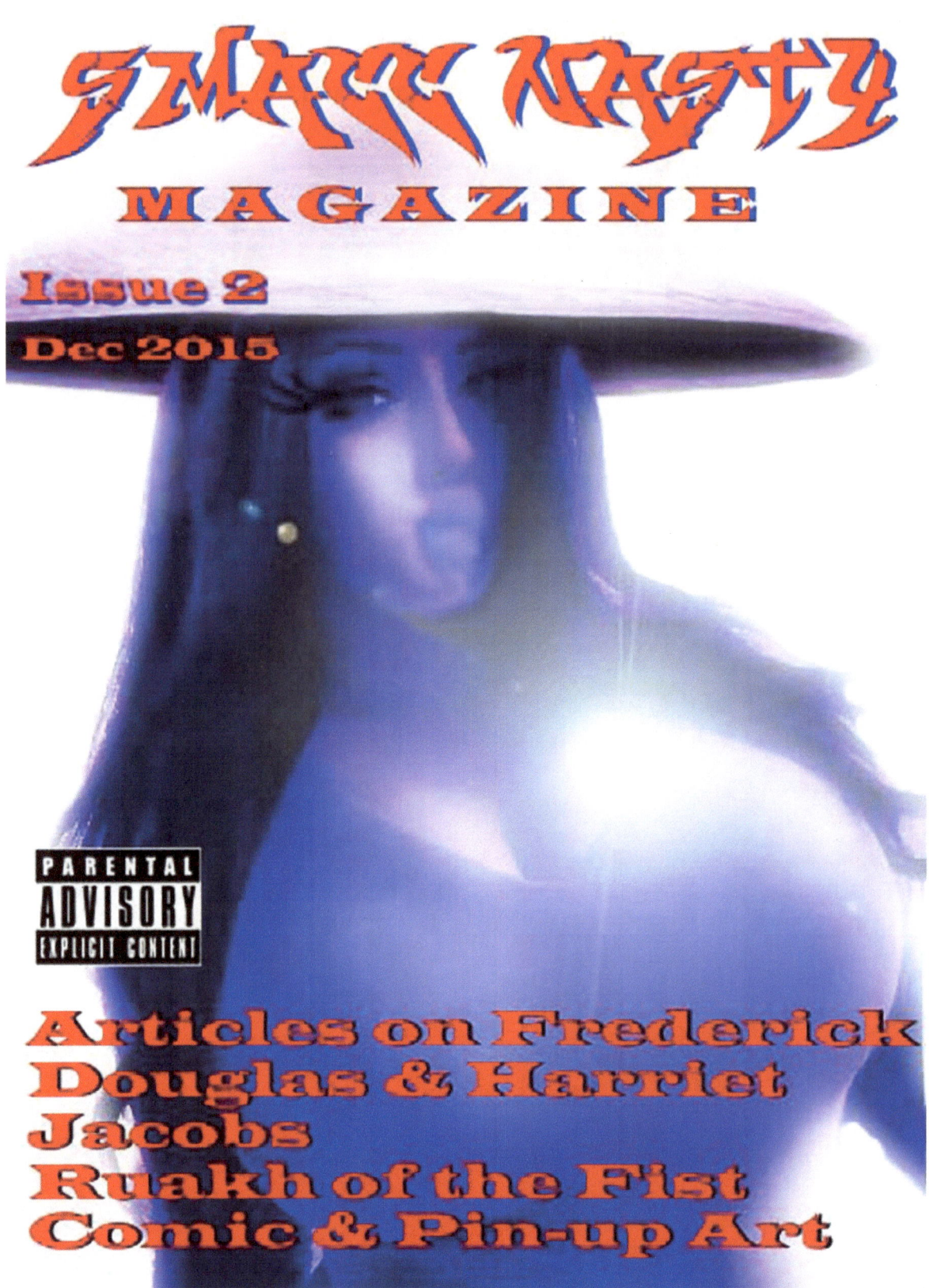

SMACK NASTY

MAGAZINE

Issue 2

Dec 2015

PARENTAL
ADVISORY
EXPLICIT CONTENT

Articles on Frederick
Douglas & Harriet
Jacobs
Ruakh of the Fist
Comic & Pin-up Art

www.smaccnasty.com

www.facebook.com/smaccnastycorporation

Contact: smaccnasty@yahoo.com

www.ingramcontent.com/pod-product-compliance
Lightning Source LLC
Chambersburg PA
CBHW040743200526
45159CB00023B/1607